The Culture of
A Community College

Preface by
Everett C. Hughes

The Culture of
A Community College

Howard B. London

PRAEGER PUBLISHERS
Praeger Special Studies

New York   •   London   •   Sydney   •   Toronto

Library of Congress Cataloging in Publication Data

London, Howard B
    The culture of a community college.

    Bibliography: p.
    1. Community colleges—United States. 2. United
States—Intellectual life. 3. Education, Humanistic—
United States. 4. College students' socio-economic
status—United States. I. Title.
LB2328.L58   378.1'543'0973   78-8697
ISBN 0-03-044701-1

PRAEGER PUBLISHERS, PRAEGER SPECIAL STUDIES
383 Madison Avenue, New York, N.Y., 10017, U.S.A.
Published in the United States of America in 1978
by Praeger Publishers,
A Division of Holt, Rinehart and Winston, CBS Inc.
89 038 987654321

For Everett C. Hughes

PREFACE

In modern societies, children are made to attend formal organized schools following a calendar and a curriculum set by some combination of state, church, family, and/or popular authority. The child starts school not long after she or he can be comfortably separated from the parents for several hours at a time. In simpler economies, the girl continues until the mother wants her at home to help; the boy, until the father wants him in his field or shop. In the American village schools that I attended, some boys left school to help their ditch-digging fathers as soon as the frost was out of the ground in the spring. A son might start high school at the age of 14, struggle with *amo, amas, amat* for a few weeks until October corn-cutting began, and come back for a few weeks in midwinter; he might also "quit" school and go to work. The doubtful status of "dropout" did not exist. By the last year of high school, there remained only the doctor's daughter, the preacher's sons, the children of the more prosperous merchants, a couple of children of well-to-do farmers, and a bright girl or two who would go on to normal school in order to teach in the country until she married.

As the roads got better, children finished grammar school and buses brought them in to centralized high schools. In cities the Catholic parochial system developed alongside public schools. Immigrant parents got caught in the old trap: how long must we keep these children in school and get no income from them? Public school was free, but food and shoes were not. Eventually, nearly all children stayed in school until adolescence; that is, children who were clean, decently dressed, moderately well behaved, and healthy. The lame, the deaf, the blind, the feeble-minded, and the troublesome were either kept at home or "sent away" to special institutions. In every community, a few children were kept at home because of chronic illness, usually tuberculosis; when one died, all were marched from school to attend the funeral. Eventually, provision was made in many communities for the transport to school of crippled children and heart patients and the schools themselves were made safer for handicapped pupils.

Urban industrial society made school available to all from a very early age, keeping children there through mid-adolescence. Schools were now looking after the children of mothers who worked as well as of those who did not. Many of them were actually in custody, kept whether they were learning or not—although, of course they were all learning. They learned what their teachers and parents wanted them to learn as well as much that the authorities and parents did not necessarily want them to learn. Indeed, they learned how to survive wherever they lived; but survival on the street is not taught in school.

In industrial populations where the trade apprenticeship system prevailed, leaving school was coordinated with entry into an apprenticeship. The apprentice was supposed to be a learner; he was also a part-time worker and was initiated into a peer group. Apprenticeship, even in the proud trade of shipbuilding, is not flourishing today, and many of the students in the urban community college are sons of men who have lost their faith in apprenticeship and thus want their children to stay at school longer. The "school" after the secondary level is often the community college, the most rapidly growing part of our "higher educational" system. It is one thing to want to go to school and another to want to do the things one must do to succeed there; this is, in effect, a main finding of Howard London's study. In the past, the young adults staying in universities already had middle-class habits. One of the things required of a middle-class child is solitary book study. Not all of them like this very much, but they learn to do it. As Allison Davis found in Chicago, a working-class boy is considered selfish if he goes away to study by himself; they, and their fathers, like to go to the pub in a group. College boys like that too—the much maligned college fraternity set someone to watch over them so that they would spend at least an hour or two at lonely study after dinner. Men attending night law school gather in one another's houses to study in groups, while their wives make refreshments and coffee in the kitchen. These varied kinds of study are as much a matter of life style as of subject matter. As we have more and more kinds of schools, and people of every age and condition going to school, we will need knowledge of a variety of life styles interacting with the subject matter of education.

Howard London has given us an excellent analysis of the problems both of keeping young adults in school longer than used to be customary, and doing it in circumstances quite alien to the student's peer culture. It takes exactly this kind of field observation, with careful note-taking, to get this kind of knowledge. The U.S. community college is introducing more young people to a new style of learning and living than any institution has ever done. I hope that *The Culture of a Community College* will be read not only as a work manual to be followed, but also as an interesting slice of American life.

Everett C. Hughes
Boston College
28 March 1978

ACKNOWLEDGMENTS

This research reflects the influence and enlightenment of many persons. My parents must be thanked first, for it was they who nurtured me in love and concern for others. I am also profoundly indebted to the students, teachers, and administrators of City Community College for their cooperation and willingness to take me into their lives. To Shirley Urban, who helped type the field notes, and to Betty Green, who typed the manuscript and offered many practical suggestions, I owe many thanks.

It was in a seminar in my last year at Bowdoin College that I was first drawn to the study of higher education; I would not have been so captivated were it not for the wonderful teaching of William Whiteside. John Donovan, Michael Malec, and David Karp provided further intellectual stimulation and colleagueship during my graduate school days, and I shall always be most grateful to them. Although I did not have the pleasure of meeting David Riesman and Burton Clark until after this book was written, their work has always been most informative and provocative.

To my dear friend and colleague Thomas Ktsanes, whose constructive criticisms of this research, to say nothing of life itself, have helped in so many ways, thank you from the bottom of my heart. Finally, this work is affectionately dedicated to Everett C. Hughes, whose sociological vision, curiosity, and compassion have incalculably enriched my life.

CONTENTS

LIST OF TABLES AND FIGURES

INTRODUCTION

> All of the available evidence indicates that the disadvantaged student
> and the slow learner like education and see its value. The evidence
> also indicates that these students often hate school.
>
> > William Moore, Jr.
> > *Against the Odds: The*
> > *High Risk Student in*
> > *the Community College*

In the past 15 years, the most radical structural change in higher
education has been the remarkable growth of community colleges.
Since 1960, the number of community college students in degree credit
programs has quintupled from 451,000 to 2.5 million; these students
now account for over one third of all undergraduates in this country.[1]
During these same years the number of two-year colleges with degree
credit programs almost doubled from 521 in 1960 to 974 in 1975.[2] This
study is a field investigation of the culture of one community college
and how that culture is related to the larger social system in which it
exists.

There are, of course, several kinds of community and junior colleges.[3] Public two-year institutions are formally controlled either by
municipal, county, or state governments. Some are specialized technical and agricultural schools, while others offer a variety of career programs. The private junior colleges are equally diverse. Some are
coeducational, others enroll only males or females, and some are either
affiliated with the Catholic church or a Protestant denomination.
Whether public or private, junior colleges vary in size, objectives, curricula, tuition, living accommodations, faculty backgrounds, and socioeconomic status of students.

The community college studied in this report is representative in
many ways of the kind of community college that is growing faster
than any other.[4] It is urban, offers several career programs as well as
a liberal arts transfer curriculum, and is attended predominantly by
students who are white and working class, have low levels of educational achievement, and commute from nearby neighborhoods.[5] Despite the growing importance of such institutions, there are no
systematic studies of what happens on a day-to-day basis in them or
how their internal workings relate to outside cultural influences. This
ethnography was designed to fill that gap. Most simply, the basic research problem was to discover the kind of college community the new
community college is.

Investigating this problem required learning the working definitions of community college life used by students and teachers to order their behavior. Because the fieldwork coincided with the school's opening, the central ethnographic effort was to discover those factors that most influenced the development of these working definitions. To understand better what is meant by "working definitions," it is necessary to consider both the theory (symbolic interaction) that postulates their existence and efficacy and the method (participant observation) by which they are uncovered.

As developed by George Herbert Mead, John Dewey, Charles Horton Cooley, and Robert Park, symbolic interaction focuses on the shared meanings of actions and how people organize or mesh their activity with reference to those shared meanings. Sociology, from this point of view, is the study of these collective actions—the forms they take; the conditions under which they arise, change, or disappear; and their consequences for group life.[6] The central theoretical concept is that an individual can imagine how his actions will be interpreted by others and is thus able continually to organize and reorganize his behavior by taking into account the anticipated and actual responses of others. Interaction is seen as symbolic, as, through this role taking, actions are infused with a shared subjective meaning that they otherwise do not have.

Collective actions flowing from this process and the attitudes people come to have concerning them do not exist in a vacuum, but emerge in and are part of larger social networks. In other words, whatever people do they are constrained by situations, circumstances, and events not entirely of their own making. They may act back upon them and so influence and change a given social world (in this case, a community college), but complete freedom and autonomy of action are incompatible with sociological theory in general and symbolic interaction in particular. As George Herbert Mead stated in his discussion of the "generalized other":

> The self-conscious human individual, then, takes or assumes the organized social attitudes of the given social group or community (or of some one section thereof) to which he belongs, toward the social problems of various kinds which confront that group or community at any given time and which arise in connection with the correspondingly different social projects or organized cooperative enterprises in which that group or community as such is engaged; and as an individual participant in these social projects or cooperative enterprises, he governs his own conduct accordingly.[7]

Mead, then, states that when people orient their behavior in response to the constraints or demands posed by various social agencies and circumstances, that is, when people see themselves sharing similar goals and problems in a common situation, there develops a "working definition," or "perspective" as it will be called in this book. (The relationship between what people come to appreciate as problematic and the ideology in which that occurs is discussed throughout this volume.)

Since Mead, the concept of perspective has been used by many theorists and researchers. Karl Mannheim defined perspective as "the subject's whole mode of conceiving things as determined by his historical and social setting."[8] Mannheim also emphasized that perspectives are a group phenomenon:

> They [perspectives] do not have their origin in the first place in the individual's becoming aware of his interests in the course of his thinking. Rather, *they arise out of the collective purposes of a group* which underlie the thought of the individual. . . . In this connection, it becomes more clear that a large part of thinking and knowing cannot be correctly understood, as long as its connection with existence or with the social implications of human life are not taken into account.[9]

Tamotsu Shibutani defines "perspectives" and stresses their functions:

> A perspective is an ordered view of one's world—what is taken for granted about the attributes of various objects, events and human nature. It is an order of things remembered and expected as well as things actually perceived, an organized conception of what is plausible; it constitutes the matrix through which one perceives his environment. The fact that men have such ordered perspectives enables them to conceive of their ever changing world as relatively stable, orderly and predictable . . . one's perspective is an outline scheme which, running ahead of experience, defines and guides it.[10]

Although Mannheim and Shibutani did not include actions in their definitions of perspectives, a number of researchers have investigated the relationship between the two. For example, Everett Hughes, Howard Becker, Blanche Geer, and Anselm Strauss have explicitly analyzed perspectives and their relationships to group behavior in two student cultures, a medical school and an undergraduate college.[11] Their conception is similar to Mead's in that perspectives are seen as providing views, motives, and strategies:

> We use the term "perspective" to refer to a coordinated set of ideas and actions a person uses in dealing with some problematic situation. . . . These thoughts and actions are coordinated in the sense that

the actions flow reasonably, from the actor's point of view, from the ideas contained in the perspective. Similarly, the ideas can be seen by an observer to be one of the possible sets of ideas which might form the underlying rationale for the person's actions and are seen by the actor as providing a justification for acting as he does.[12]

A perspective, to be more precise, contains several elements: a definition of the situation in which the actors are involved, a statement of the goals they are trying to achieve, a set of ideas specifying what kinds of activities are expedient and proper, and a set of activities or practices congruent with them.[13]

Although not explicitly using the concept of perspective, ethnographers such as William Foote Whyte,[14] Elliot Liebow,[15] and David Sudnow[16] attempt to show how perspectives and actions flowing from them were created during the course of daily life in response to the problems designated in their books. In addition, they relate their subjects' perspectives to various professional, institutional, community, and historical contingencies and pressures.

Similarly, in this investigation of the urban community college, perspectives are seen both as arising from daily exigencies and as being articulated with more distant phenomena, such as career paths, technological advances, social class, the ideology of individual self-determination, and the status of the community college itself. The very task and promise of sociology, said C. Wright Mills, are to understand such intersections of biography and history.[17] The sociological imagination, he said, "is the capacity to range from the most impersonal and remote transformations to the most intimate features of the human self—and to see the relations between the two."[18] Hopefully, this study contains some of this sociological imagination.

Given the exploratory nature of this undertaking (this is the first ethnographic study of a community college known to the author), hypotheses were not formed in advance. There were two reasons for this. First, at the outset of the study the only thing that could be said with certainty about the significant variables was that they were the "conditions of life" around which the actors' perspectives would evolve.[19] Because the field did not yet exist, neither the significant variables nor the content of the perspectives could be known. To have hypothesized at this stage would have required the very knowledge the study was designed to secure.[20] As with the ethnographies cited above, the purpose of this study was not to test hypotheses, but to uncover some rather basic knowledge of a group's culture.

Second, as Herbert Blumer implies, one of the advantages of this approach is to increase the researcher's capacity for surprise by maximizing the opportunity for discovering that understandings, images, and hypotheses of a particular world under study are somehow erroneous and must be reformulated:

> The modes of living of ... groups, the parade of situations they must handle, their institutions and their organizations, the relations between their members, the views and images through which they see their worlds, the personal organizations formed by their members—all these and more reflect their different empirical worlds. One should not blind oneself to a recognition of the fact that human beings in carrying on their collective life form very different kinds of worlds. To study them intelligently one has to know these worlds, and to know the worlds one has to examine them closely. No theorizing, however ingenious, and no observance of scientific protocol, however meticulous, substitutes for developing a familiarity with what is actually going on in the sphere of life under study. . . . The task of scientific study is to lift the veils that cover the area of group life that one proposes to study. The veils are not lifted by substituting preformed images for firsthand knowledge. The veils are lifted by getting close to the area and by digging deep into it through careful study. Schemes of methodology that do not encourage or allow this betray the cardinal principle of respecting the nature of one's empirical world.[21]

With these cautions in mind, the data were collected during one academic year (1973–74) of participant observation. The main body of data is a record of the day-to-day experiences and comments of students and teachers in classrooms, lounges, corridors, stairwells, offices, cafeteria, and the surrounding campus and local bars and shops. Two other sources of data were tape-recorded interviews of teachers and various records and statistics compiled by school officials. Methodological procedures and problems are detailed in Appendix A.

NOTES

1. U.S., Department of Health, Education, and Welfare, *The Digest of Educational Statistics, 1975–1976.* (Washington, D.C.: U.S. Government Printing Office, 1976), p. 96.
2. Ibid.
3. The titles "junior" and "community" are used interchangeably. The trend in the past 15 years has been toward "community college," as "junior college" signifies an inferior status. Two-year college administrators increasingly want their institutions to be seen not as "less than" but "different from" four-year colleges and universities. On this point see Thomas E. O'Connell, *Community Colleges: A President's View* (Urbana, Ill.: University of Illinois Press, 1968), Ch. 3, pp. 34–53.
4. K. Patricia Cross, *Beyond the Open Door: New Students to Higher Education* (San Francisco: Jossey-Bass, 1971), pp. 15–16.
5. Ibid.

6. Howard S. Becker, Blanche Geer, and Everett C. Hughes, *Making the Grade: The Academic Side of College Life* (New York: Wiley, 1968), p. 5.

7. Anselm Strauss, ed., *George Herbert Mead on Social Psychology: Selected Papers* (Chicago: University of Chicago Press, 1964), pp. 220–21.

8. Karl Mannheim, *Ideology and Utopia: An Introduction to the Sociology of Knowledge* (New York: Harcourt, Brace, 1936), p. 239.

9. Ibid., pp. 240–41; emphasis added.

10. Tamotsu Shibutani, "Reference Groups as Perspectives," *American Journal of Sociology* 60 (May 1955): 564.

11. Howard S. Becker, Blanche Geer, Everett C. Hughes, and Anselm Strauss, *Boys in White: Student Culture in Medical School* (Chicago: University of Chicago Press, 1961); Beckes, Geer, and Hughes, *Making the Grade.*

12. Becker, Geer, Hughes, and Strauss, *Boys in White,* p. 34.

13. Ibid., p. 436.

14. William Foote Whyte, *Street Corner Society: The Social Structure of an Italian Slum* (Chicago: University of Chicago Press, 1943).

15. Elliot Liebow, *Tally's Corner: A Study of Negro Streetcorner Men* (Boston: Little, Brown, 1967).

16. David Sudnow, *Passing On: The Social Organization of Dying* (Englewood Cliffs, N.J.: Prentice-Hall, 1967).

17. C. Wright Mills, *The Sociological Imagination* (New York: Oxford University Press, 1959), p. 6.

18. Ibid., p. 7.

19. Herbert Blumer, "Sociological Implications of the Thought of George Herbert Mead," *American Journal of Sociology* 71 (March 1966): 541.

20. Herbert Blumer, *Symbolic Interactionism: Perspective and Method* (Englewood Cliffs, N.J.: Prentice-Hall, 1969), p. 37. For example, it was not possible at the outset to know to what extent social class would influence students' perspectives or what the relationship might be between teachers' career paths and their perspectives. Indeed, the significance of these variables was discovered during the course of the investigation.

21. Ibid., p. 39.

The Culture of
A Community College

1
SOCIAL CLASS
AND THE STUDENT BODY

City Community College (CCC) is situated in a major urban complex in the northeastern United States. As do most community colleges, it offers both liberal arts and vocational curricula. The Liberal Arts Program is designed for students who plan "to earn the degree of Bachelor of Arts or Sciences from a four year college or university" (City Community College catalog). Among the requirements are courses in the humanities, mathematics, natural sciences, and social sciences.

The five career programs are "designed to provide a general education background plus a definite occupational skill so that the student may seek employment in a semiprofessional or technical career at the end of the two year program" (City Community College catalog). (In addition to the required English and vocational courses, students in these curricula also have to choose among designated liberal arts electives.) The Executive Secretary Program combines liberal arts, business, and secretarial courses to prepare students as office secretaries. The Business Administration Program requires courses in basic accounting and mathematics as well as in marketing, management, business law, and social science. The Human Services Program is "intended to prepare students as assistants to professionals in careers that direct the delivery of services to people. These fields include Social Welfare, Mental Health, Community Development, Administration, Child Care and Teacher Aide and/or Teacher Assistant" (City Community College catalog). Courses are required in mathematics, the social sciences, political science, counseling methods, and interview techniques; during the second year students are to arrange an intern experience.

The Law Enforcement Program is designed to prepare graduates for employment in public and private law enforcement and security agencies. Among the required courses are principles of evidence, urban society, criminal law, state and local government, traffic and patrol procedures, and criminal investigations, as well as others pertinent to on-the-job knowledge and skills. The Fire Protection and Safety Technology Program prepares students as firemen or business and industrial safety technicians. Required courses include fire protection, fire prevention, building construction, fire protection systems and equipment, hazardous materials, basic chemistry, and urban society. In addition are a number of electives, such as fire fighting tactics and strategy, fire codes and ordinances, and fire company officership.

During its first year the school enrolled 1,103 full-time students. An institutional questionnaire designed to assess their socioeconomic status was returned by so few students (less than 25 percent) that the results are not included in this report. However, data culled from students' records show that 7.5 percent (82 students) of CCC's first class were from the community in which the school is located and 67.5 percent (745) were from 13 adjacent or nearby communities (a total of 75 percent). Figures 1.1 through 1.5 offer comparative data on the 14 communities in which 75 percent of the students lived. (The remaining communities are discussed below.) Figure 1.1 shows the population of the Standard Statistical Metropolitan Area (SMSA), the population of each community, and the percentage of the student body from each community.*

Figures 1.2 and 1.3 show the percentages of high school and college graduates among people over 25 years old in each community. Compared to the SMSA, the 14 communities have from 8 to 33 percent fewer high school graduates; in half the communities less than 40 percent have high school diplomas. (As stated in Figure 1.1, Community D is becoming increasingly black. The percentage of high school graduates in the black census tracts (over 50 percent black) is also 35 percent.) Similarly, these communities lag behind the SMSA in the percentage of college graduates; with one exception, they trail by 6 to 14 percent and in half the communities, 5 percent or less have bachelor's degrees. (The percentage of college graduates in the black census tracts in Community D is only slightly lower than in the white tracts—1.5 percent.)

Figure 1.4 shows that 13 of the 14 communities have median family incomes below that for the SMSA; half the communities have median incomes 16 to 26 percent less than the SMSA. (While the educational levels of the black and white census tracts of community D are equal, the median family income in the black tracts is only $6,335, or 28 percent lower. Although incidental to this study, these statistics are

---

*The data in Figures 1 through 5 are from the U.S. Bureau of the Census, *1970 Census of Population and Housing.* Communities B through F are communities within the geopolitical boundaries of the major city (A) as determined by custom and as reflected in the census tracts. G through N are satellite cities and towns.

FIGURE 1.1: Population of 14 Communities

Community	Percentage of CCC Student Body	Population
SMSA		2,754,000
A	(6.8)	437,000
B	(7.4)	15,000
C	(4.9)	39,000
D	(4.0)	67,000*
E	(2.4)	38,000
F	(1.8)	11,000
G	(3.7)	100,000
H	(4.0)	31,000
I	(8.0)	42,000
J	(7.2)	56,000
K	(8.0)	64,000
L	(2.7)	43,000
M	(9.1)	89,000
N	(4.4)	33,000

*The northern and western census tracts of Community D have become increasingly populated by blacks over the past 10 years; 33.66 percent of its population of 101,346 is black. As no black students from this area attended CCC, only white census tracts were used to compute the statistics on this and the following graphs. Defining a white census tract as any tract over 50 percent white, there are 15 such tracts in Community D; only 7.8 percent of the people in these 15 tracts are black.

Source: U.S. Bureau of the Census, 1970.

yet another indication that blacks with an equal number of years education do not earn an equivalent income.) Figure 1.5 indicates that, compared to the SMSA, 10 of the 14 communities have from 66 to 78 percent fewer black people; in half the communities black people are less

FIGURE 1.2: Percentage of High School Graduates of Population over 25 Years Old in 14 Communities

Community	Percentage of High School Graduates of Population over 25 Years Old
SMSA	63
A	55
B	45
C	36
D	35
E	43
F	30
G	34
H	35
I	41
J	38
K	48
L	46
M	38
N	44

Source: U.S. Bureau of the Census, 1970.

than 1.1 percent of the population. (The 7.8 percent figure for Community D represents only those blacks who live in census tracts over 50 percent white.) Taken together, the data in Tables 1.1 through 1.5 show that 75 percent of the students come from predominantly white, less educated, and lower-income communities.

Of the 25 percent not from the major service area, 15 percent are from contiguous communities, 8 percent are from 48 cities and towns within the state, and 2 percent are from 6 other states and 2 foreign nations. Eliminating the other states and nations, most of these areas

FIGURE 1.3: Percentage of College Graduates of Population over 25 Years Old in 14 Communities

Community	Percentage of College (Four-Year) Graduates of Population over 25 Years Old
SMSA	16
A	10
B	9
C	8
D	2
E	8
F	9
G	10
H	4
I	5
J	4
K	4
L	5
M	2
N	16

Source: U.S. Bureau of the Census, 1970.

are suburban, better educated, and have higher median incomes and higher proportions of the population engaged in white-collar work.[1]

The data analysis presented thus far is based on the assumption that students share the social characteristics of their communities. For example, while 75 percent of CCC students were from 14 less educated, lower-income, blue-collar communities, it is another matter to state that the students' families share these characteristics. The data are not individual but ecological, and any observations made from them must be premised on the contextual effects of living in such communities.

Certainly, ecological data are important even when they do not reflect individual data, but it can be a mistake to substitute unthinkingly one for the other.[2]

Although the school's data on students' socioeconomic status were inadequate, data gathered in the field indicated that most students were indeed from the kind of family described above. The best "hard" socioeconomic data gathered in the field were fathers' occupations (discussed below). Many data were gathered, however, on the nonquantifiable components of social and economic standing. I am talking here of class culture. The students' class culture, how they feel about and live within that culture, and the consequences of feeling and living that

FIGURE 1.4: Median Family Income for 14 Communities

Community	Median Family Income
SMSA	$11,400
A	9,800
B	8,800
C	8,600
D	8,800
E	8,700
F	8,400
G	9,800
H	9,000
I	10,000
J	10,200
K	11,000
L	10,300
M	9,600
N	12,400

Source: U.S. Bureau of the Census, 1970.

FIGURE 1.5:   Percentage of Black Population in 14 Communities

Communities	Percentage of Black Population
SMSA	4.6
A	10.8
B	0.1
C	0.2
D	7.8
E	0.1
F	0.2
G	6.8
H	1.7
I	1.3
J	1.3
K	2.5
L	0.1
M	1.1
N	0.9

Source: U.S. Bureau of the Census, 1970.

way in the context of the community college are the "soft" data of this study. These data are no less important in sociological study; in this investigation they are essential to the understanding of the inner life of City Community College.

That the majority of students were from working-class families was learned in several ways: in conversations and interviews with students, in passing remarks made in classes, in social science classes where students were asked to discuss their socioeconomic status, and in formal interviews with teachers and administrators. The students' fathers typically had such blue-collar occupations as construction worker, telephone worker, longshoreman, mechanic, electrician, policeman, plumber, fork-lift driver, truck driver, industrial machinist, or municipal or state worker. Approximately 15 percent of students' fathers had white-collar occupations in the lower levels of large bureaucracies, for example, postal clerk, probation officer, and state or town office worker. Some students, approximately 5 percent, were clearly middle-class in that one or both parents had a college education, lived in an affluent community, and had such occupations as high state or corporate official, lawyer, or owner of a retail business.

Most students, however, lived in neighborhoods where narrow, pale houses and tenements were packed in tight rows, with perhaps a postage-stamp yard in front or back. They were frequently adjacent to industrial areas where the landscape was woven with chain link fences and punctured with hulking, dreary buildings and smokestacks. In other neighborhoods the homes were not as old or as tall, but they were almost all two-family. From the school itself some two dozen smokestacks were visible as were warehouses, piles of scrap metal and junk, a plot of new low-income modular housing, tenement rows, church spires, two historical monuments, and a complex of major commuter and truck highways that passed not through, but over, the community. A short walk from the school was the rapid transit line, where steel wheels screeched on elevated tracks. (The school was designed architecturally to protect students from the urban noise. The physical structure is depicted in Appendix B.)

On several occasions I drove students home and was invited in, and usually up. Peter Binzen's description of "Whitetown" homes captures the flavor of these dwellings:

> The television set is a big new color model. The house is neat and better furnished than its plain gray exterior would lead one to expect. On the wall behind the TV is a proud affirmation in needlepoint: A MAN'S HOME IS HIS CASTLE. On the kitchen wall is the prayerful GOD BLESS OUR HOME. In both rooms are religious ornaments and bouquets of plastic flowers.[3]

Perhaps the most important point here is that CCC students lived with their parents.* Most students could not afford to move from their families, but beyond that there was no felt need to move. Little else in their lives had changed other than that they were going to to local

---

*Students who had their own apartments or homes were usually older or married. The older students, a relatively small group, but one with a different perspective, are described in Chapter 4.

school. They kept the same afternoon and evening jobs they had in high school, the same set of friends, and the same lifestyle.

Status passage was minimal, for old relationships were barely upset. As one student stated:

> "Why should I [move]? I have everything where I want it." He adds he and Tony and Louie thought about getting an apartment near the school a couple of weeks ago and splitting the rent. "We didn't think it was worth it. It's not like our parents tell us to be in at twelve." I ask him if he just would like the feeling of being out on his own. He says, "I already am. I was all through high school. The only time my parents gave me shit was when I got into trouble at school and then I'd just stay at Louie's."

In short, he was not "going away to college" and there was no apprehension about being uprooted from the local community and the local social system. This was even more common among female students, as in the ethnic neighborhoods (discussed below) females were more protected and sheltered:

> Walters [a social science teacher] asks if they have had experiences which resemble those described in the textbook. One Italian girl from _____ [the Italian section of the city] says she comes from a very traditional family and that her sister had to go out with a boy for six years before her parents would allow her to accept an engagement ring. The family insisted they move very slowly.

In another social science class, the following incident occurred:

> The class discusses patriarchalism; they [a clique of four females from the Irish section] say their fathers are very dominant and protective.
>
> First female: "My father eats in the living room, but we can't. I don't buy that—who does he think he is?"
>
> Two of her friends respond immediately and simultaneously, "He's your father!"
>
> First female: "Well, how do you like it, Jan, when your father tells you to be in at 12? You're always moanin' about that."
>
> Jan: "Whew, my parents are strict as hell. If I ever came home drunk, they'd kill me. That's why they didn't want me to go to _____ [the state university]."

In addition to living with their families, many students came to CCC with a clique of neighborhood or high school friends. This was evident during the four days of registration when friends were reunited after the summer or arrived together in small groups. They discussed their vacations, high school tales, and the confusing registration process. For many students the old gang was still together.

The supportive network of family and friends was strengthened by ethnic affiliations. Four of the 14 communities have distinct ethnic identities and reputations; ethnic foods, customs, and celebrations are a way of life in Communities B and E (predominantly Irish) and C and F (predominantly Italian). In the seven communities arcing CCC (G, H, I, J, K, L, and N) the Irish and the Italians are the largest groups, with a sprinkling of French-Canadians, Jews, Poles, and Armenians contributing to the ethnic mix.

The ethnicity of the students themselves was difficult to determine.* The ethnicity of their names was surmised from a roster supplied by the school administration; names were categorized only if they were distinctly ethnic. The ethnicity of names was also recorded in the 39 instances of teachers' calling class rolls (of a total of 391 classes observed). Because names are an inadequate and frequently misleading expression of ethnicity, the following percentages are only very crude indicators: Irish 45 percent; Italian 40 percent; and Jewish, French-Canadian, Polish, Greek, and Armenian were spread more or less evenly among the remaining 15 percent.† While these 15 percent majored in diverse subjects, the Law Enforcement and Fire Science programs were almost exclusively Irish and Italian.

Despite the students' urban environment, their range of experiences and interests was limited—they were urban but not urbane. (This generalization does not apply to a small group of older students who are described separately in Chapter 4.) Despite their proximity to a major intellectual center with numerous public cultural events and facilities, the students were unfamiliar with stage theater, art museums, libraries, and symphonies. Their most popular movies were *The Poseidon Adventure, The Godfather, The Exorcist,* and police shows, such as *The New Centurions* and *The Blue Knight.* Despite a number of art and foreign film theaters in the nearby university section, it was not the students' style to attend.[4]

---

*Students' ethnic background was asked for on the same school questionnaire described earlier. Too few were returned for the information to be useful.

†Discussions with four Ethiopian students revealed they had relatives teaching in or attending nearby universities. Two Ethiopians were attending CCC because they arrived in America too late to be admitted to any school without an open admissions policy; one enrolled because his father knew one of the teachers at CCC and wanted an eye kept on his son, and the last enrolled because he did not feel ready for "a real American college" and was told a community college would help prepare him.

News magazines were seldom read, as illustrated by this incident that occurred in the first English class of the second semester:

> Weiss [the teacher] asks them to imagine they are on a desert island, and a man, appearing from a huge scallop shell, says they will be trapped on the island for the next 10 years. But they can subscribe to two magazines, one a news magazine, the other any kind of magazine; they are asked to write down their choices. A number of students give each other what appear to be looks of disgust with the teacher. . . . As we leave the classroom there is a great deal of laughter and kidding. Bill asks Steve which magazine he chose. Steve put down *Time* and *Penthouse.*
>
> Bill: "You're shitting! You put down *Time* magazine?"
>
> Steve: "Hey, you gotta get in good with the teacher." As it turned out Bill, Tony, Louie, and Frank all put down *Time* or *Newsweek,* but read neither.
>
> Tony says, "Maybe we should have put down *Weekly Reader.*" They laugh. I ask what they do read. Frank says that once in a great while he'll go to the school library to read *Newsweek,* but will read only "the good stuff . . . you know, the sports and the stuff near the back."

Their chief extraschool experience was work. Over 80 percent of the males had part- or full-time manual jobs; most common were stockroom work, loading and unloading, delivering, cleaning, and cashiering. One motive for working was to have a car for the girlfriend it might bring and so was both a status symbol and an assertion of masculinity. Approximately 20 percent of the female students were employed, most often as waitresses and cashiers. Most also helped in the home by caring for younger children and helping with the cleaning and cooking. That fewer females owned automobiles created something of a vicious circle. Without jobs they could not support cars and without cars they had difficulty finding and keeping jobs. In this way the females were kept captive in the family while the males were not.*

The students at CCC tended to be conservative in their personal and political values and beliefs. This is consistent with national survey findings that show urban community college students more frequently exhibit authoritarian personality traits and are "less attracted to reflexive thought and less tolerant than their peers in four year institutions."[5] This was especially clear in the students' strident racism:

---

*Suggested in a correspondence from David Riesman.

> They [a group of male law enforcement students] discuss the one black male in the Law Enforcement program.
>
> George says, "This morning he says to us, 'Anytime you want to take me on, go right ahead!'"
>
> Joe replies: "Hell, it would be 40 to 1." He pulls a knife from his jacket and adds: "He says we can't talk about them [blacks] that way? When I have this I can."
>
> (hallway conversation)

> The [class] discussion turns to why blacks are not in certain organizations—fire, police, transit, trade unions. It is the male students who do the talking. They say it's because blacks are lazy, they don't want to work. [The instructor] tries to rationally explain the constraints faced by blacks. . . . He fails to reduce their animosity; his arguments only make the students more vehement.
>
> (a social science class)

> As five black students walk by, they [white students] "hate stare" them and make derogatory remarks about their dashikis and afros. They call them "jungle bunnies" and then mimic black speech.
>
> (cafeteria conversation)

The standard clothing for males was jeans (usually blue) and colored jerseys or shirts; most females dressed in blue jeans and blouses or sweaters. It was as rare to see a male in a sport jacket as it was to see a female in a skirt. As discussed below, the popularity of blue jeans and work clothes was not a symbol of disdain for respectability or upward mobility as once was the case on college campuses; because these students did not have to work at identifying with "common" people, it was the clothes and not the ideas behind them that were fashionable. For those who worked before or after school these clothes were simply practical.

Very few males wore mustaches and only three wore beards. Most wore their hair well below the ears (with the exception of the firemen, who were prohibited by occupation), although a few clung to the "DA" style, popular in the 1950s and early 1960s. Having one's hair styled in a more contemporary fashion prompted peer comments such as:

> Hey, finally moving out of _____ [the name of the student's neighborhood].

> Faaan——cy. If you keep your mouth shut maybe you can score with Raquel Welch.

Both comments associate image change with status change; the first comment refers to a new and presumably better neighborhood, the second to access to a new and higher circle of women. As discussed in Chapters 3 and 4, status passage was very much on students' minds.

As do their counterparts across the nation, most CCC students had poor academic histories;[6] undoubtedly, many of their schools have not served them well. A school administrator estimated that 25 to 30 percent of the student body were denied admission by four-year colleges and universities and another 5 percent had withdrawn from senior colleges for academic reasons. In an interview she further stated:

> The law enforcement majors were underachievers and had a lot of trouble in high school. Their range of scores on the SATs was from 200 to 350. The liberal arts people scored higher but the very few who got over 500 or 600 are from your suburban schools.... We have maybe 10 or 12 who did that well. But it's the law enforcement kids, they're the group. Most of them are young, they just got out of high school. They're psychological misfits. They mostly failed in high school.
>
> (an administrator)

The administrators, of course, expected unsuccessful and high-risk students and had established a "Learning Center," one function of which was remedial education. In the words of the center's director:

> Most of the students come from very poor high schools. On the pretests we gave them most of them tested out at seventh and eighth grade reading levels and math skills.... Unless they came from a school system like _____ or _____ [two affluent suburbs] where these skills are emphasized, they're just not prepared.

In our society, lack of intelligence as conventionally measured by IQ tests and achievement tests is regarded as the equivalent of personal failure—especially by middle-class teachers and school administrators.[7] William Ryan has pointed out that even liberals, who are more inclined to see contextual effects, ultimately blame the student for poor performance:

> He [the student] is said to contain within himself the causes of his inability to read and write well. The shorthand phrase is "cultural deprivation," which to those in the know conveys what they allege to be inside information: that the poor child carries a scanty pack of cultural baggage as he enters the school. He doesn't know about books and magazines and newspapers they say.... In a word he is "disadvantaged" and "socially deprived," they say, and this of course, accounts for his failure (_his_ failure, they say) to learn much in school.[8]

In short, the parochialism, the poverty of personal and cultural experience, and the poor educational histories discussed in this chapter do not, in a fundamental sense, cause the students to do badly in school. The ultimate causes are to be found in the social and economic conditions that produce the victim-blaming ideology Ryan describes. As W. I. Thomas has taught us about social situations, and Karl Mannheim about social systems, whether situations be wrongly defined or ideologies myths, their consequences can be quite real. In attributing society's problems (urban decay, unresponsive educational bureaucracies, poor schools, ill-prepared and overworked teachers) to the individuals affected, these individuals are seen as inferior—lazy, undignified, unintelligent, morally and psychologically unfit ("psychological misfits").[9]

This is how the students of City Community College labeled themselves. Their working-class faith in the ethic of individualism told them that personal achievement was a matter of self-control, drive, and intelligence, so that what one does with one's life reflects one's personal virtues, flaws, and social worth:

"My family is real blue-collar," says Frank. "My father works on construction. Now what the hell can he do on a day like this. On the way in the radio said the wind chill factor is minus ten degrees. Minus ten degrees! He's fifty-five years old; he can't go on in construction much longer. And my mother's family are all longshoremen. The [union] card gets passed down. It's a tradition in some families and I know some kids who took a lot of shit because they didn't want the card. Now you take me—I worked in construction for two years after I was out of the army and I'll never forget the first day on the jackhammer. I came home, my hands all swollen and my body still shaking. After a few weeks you think nothing of it, but [he taps his chest with his finger and widens his eyes] I don't want to do that for the rest of my life. I want to better myself and I want things better for my family. So first I have to better me."

"Ya, I know," says Louie, "what is there to phys ed classes? All you have to do is organize a bunch of kids. Teaching and coaching baseball, I really think that would be a great life. To have a good job, a good family, a nice car, that's all I want. I don't want to be super wealthy, just comfortable without breaking my balls. It's just those damn biology and anatomy courses—I hate those fuckin' things. If I didn't cheat like a mother I'd never get through. Shit, it would be easy if I was smart."

"Ya, I know what you mean," says Frank.

As Frank tapped his chest there was anger and fear in the thought that he must become a "better person" to avoid living his father's life.

(The emergence and expression of anger and fear in students' perspectives are analyzed in Chapter 3.) And to have a comfortable life, Louie cheats his way through examinations in courses he hates but must pass. Both blame themselves for this condition, Frank saying his difficulties stem from not being a "better person" and Louie that things would be easy if only he were smart. Their aspirations therefore involve more than money: They seek not just a job, but a position that to them confers a sense of worth and honor.[10]

During the course of the fieldwork it became apparent that students like Frank and Louie were not part of a "deviant lower-class culture pattern," but rather had internalized some general notions of worth and success as these are defined by middle-class people and institutions. Elliot Liebow described a similar phenomenon in his analysis of the streetcorner man. His conclusion applies in part to the community college students:

> The streetcorner man does not appear as a carrier of an independent cultural tradition. His behavior appears not so much as a way of realizing the distinctive goals and values of his own subculture, or of conforming to its models, but rather as his way of trying to achieve many of the goals and values of the larger society, of failing to do this and of concealing his failure from others and from himself as best he can.[11]

Herbert Hyman makes a similar point in a survey study of the values and aspirations of different social classes:

> One systematic factor . . . which confirms at a more subtle psychological level the influence of class factors is that of the reference group of the individual. Some of our lower class individuals may well be absorbing the value system of another class to which they refer themselves.[12]

The students, then, saw themselves as *comparative* failures, for when measured against a vaguely defined middle-class reference group, they found themselves wanting.[13] Indeed, in the following excerpts from students' essays and from my field notes of their conversations, their concepts of "failure" and "personal deficiency," while not confirmed and forever ratified as they were for the men of *Tally's Corner,* were suspected. The excerpts are presented with little comment, as, when taken together, they convey a sense of the emotional climate of the school. As we shall see, this mood also was a datum.

In the first set of remarks, students' self-assessments were linked with a disquieting period in their lives in which they wandered without a clear goal or purpose. Sometimes they blamed themselves for this too:

All during high school coming to college was the furthest thing from my mind. I worked for three years while I was in high school and that really screwed up my grades, but I didn't really care. The money was good, but in a way it was worthless. I still have some nice things I bought, like my stereo, but the rest was just wasted. When I graduated I didn't want to work and like I said, college was the furthest thing from my mind. I didn't do anything except swim during the summer and then I heard about this place. So I wound up here through nobody's fault except my own.

(conversation after class)

He tells us he had a $500 scholarship to _____ University but he didn't think of going to college then: "It just wasn't in my plans. No one else in my family went to college. I wish now I would have gone." He says he has worked for his uncle in construction and then "I found out about here. I used to think I was lucky because I used to think I didn't have to go to college."

(conversation with three students in the cafeteria)

I felt for the past year and still do feel about the uncertainty of my future. I did not think too much of what I was going to do when I got out of high school because at the time, getting out of school did not seem like a reality. I did not take my school work as seriously as I should have and my attendance was poor. It finally hit me one day when I found I went from a B in Spanish to a F failure for the year. That is when I really started to think. I was off in another world the summer before my senior year at high school. I was thinking very seriously about that failure. . . . I then began to apply to various colleges. I went to my guidance counselor and he helped me a great deal in deciding what colleges were right for me. To five colleges I applied for admittance but all but one refused me. The one I was not rejected at put me on their waiting list. I went back to my guidance advisor and he told me about community and junior colleges and City Community College. He went on to explain that I do have abilities, but that I needed a little more guidance and help than other people which is not easily given at a four year college but in a Community College it is a general practice. This explains the reason why I am here.

(from a student's essay)*

---

*Errors in spelling and grammar are unchanged in all quotations from students' essays. The essays were written in the social science and English classes required of all students.

Jerry: "It's not easy getting back with it after being out of school for five years."

*HBL: "What did you do?"

Jerry: "Everything. I was in the service, worked, everything. It's really hard getting used to this."

HBL: "Getting used to what?"

Jerry: "The math. They teach it in a different way. The same thing with English. They talk about inferences, judgments, and reports. You can't just all of a sudden start thinking like that, unless you have something on the ball."

Louise: "I've been out for two years. This is the only school I could have gotten into." Jerry and Louise laugh.

(hallway conversation before class)

I ask Steve if he is in the Liberal Arts program; he says yes and adds that he thinks City Community College will be "a really nice place. . . . I was at the University of _____ [the state university] a couple of years ago. I only lasted one year." I asked why he left and he answered that it was a combination of two factors: "I'm not very good at schoolwork no matter where I go, but there it was just too impersonal. It's more personal here. I should have done better, but what the hell, that's gone."

I ask if he plans to try again when he graduates from City Community College. "I doubt it. I still don't know what I want to do. I have to find out, if I can."

(conversation in a subway after school)

Now it was off to school. First came grammar school. I breezed through their. Now the junior high, I also breezed through them. But when it came to the High school, years went slower, more homework, tougher teachers, but neverless I conquered them. I know I decided to go on to the higher education at City Community College where I am now enrolled, and plan on conquering this grade of intelligence, and this is the story of my life up and until my college days at this school. And this is my autobiography so far. I don't know what I want to be in the future. Will I find out at this school?

(from a student's essay)

My life began July 27, 1953. I weight 6½ pounds and was 21 inches long. As a child I enjoyed playing with my playmates and growing up with my family. I started school at the age of 5. School was exciting and wonderful. I had all the friends I ever needed. Then as the years went by it started to become more difficult. It was hard for me to learn and understand the basics of education. My teachers referred to me as the dreamer always in that other world. It was hard to study and conscitrat on the exact work I was doing. I sometime refer back to the days of my childhood. My childhood was my wonderland of fairyland. I live in a large family with one brother and four sisters. I am presently working at _____ [a supermarket] where I work part-times evenings. I have been working there for a year since last November. My hobbies include all sports, but I prefer baseball and hockey the most. I never played any sports in high school probably because I am too small, but I did play Babe Ruth Baseball. I was also the manager of the high school hockey team last year. I like the _____ [professional hockey team] and I watch them on television every chance I get.

The reasons I am going to college is to get a better education and to get a better job which pays more money. In college I hope to learn new things and ideas because there is no person that knows everything. The reason I chose City Community College is, well I am not that smart any ways feeling it would be easier to get into a community college rather than, lets say University of _____. Another reason is that the school is nearby and is easy to get to. I am in the Business Administration course because I am interested in business. As for my future, at the present time, I am undecided, but there is some fields that interest me, such as Accounting and I have always wanted to own my own business. As for my goals, hopes and ideas I have none at the present time.

(from a student's essay)

College life entered mine when I finally decided to go to one about a year after my high school graduation. That, up until last summer was about as far as I ever got to college. In my mind I was still undecided as to attend or not, but realizing I had nothing to lose and a bunch to gain it was off I went, and that's why I am here now. In high school my grades were poor partly because I was lazy and partly because school turned me off. I do not know what I will do with my education if I can make it through to graduate from City Community College.

(from a student's essay)

Student [reading from essay]: "I didn't have a very good background when I was younger so now I feel I have to build a respectable one and that's why I came to college."

Teacher: "What do you mean, you have to build a respectable background? Don't you respect yourself now?"

Student: "Mr. _____, every kid in this class went to a bad high school. We didn't do anything except goof off and have a great time. So to get a good job we have to come here because nobody's going to hire us unless we can point to something and say, 'See, this is what I did.' "

(from a social science class)

To begin with as a male I'm very quiet, I also know I'm very kind, understanding, and truthful. My qualities as a student are somewhat similar. I'm very, very quiet, its sometimes hard to be kind and understanding, but at least I'm still truthful. Also things are changing for me now, going to City Community College is a rather new thing to me. I'm not sure of myself, and with all the things that have been explained, I'm not sure what is to be expected of me. I'm going to miss high school, it was fun and the few years went by quickly. Now I only think about my plans for the future, finishing my two years at City Community College and transferring to _____ College [a local four year business college]. Then I'll major in Business Administration I suppose, but now I'm beginning to change my mind, wondering if this is the right career for me.

(from a student's essay)

I find it hard to study and that I give up easily, but my mother gave me a tutor. I passed every year until I finished high school. I think I didn't deserve to graduate high school because I didn't work it on my own. Anyway I am so ambitious that I want to have the best education of anybody in my hometown. Then I went to study in one of the colleges there but I flunked out. I finished a year in business administration with two courses failed and the grades were too low because I've enjoyed the company of my friends so much that sometimes I forgot my studies. So as to avoid these obstacles and control myself I rejoined my family and have come here. I hope that I can make up for the two years that I've lost.

(from a student's essay)

It was also at this time that I learned that nights were not only for studying. Like other people of my age group I started hanging around on street corners. Drinking, fighting and running around were my major pasttimes. Also at this time school lost any interest it once had for me. When school resumed, I hated it. We started getting in trouble by hooking school and cutting classes. I had to repeat my sophmore year. This was the first time I had done poorly in school and I was disappointed in myself. I resolved not to let it happen again. [Paradoxically] my only thought at this time was to get through school with as little work as possible on my part. I began to work in a bicycle shop in which I am still working in today. During my senior year in high school, I decided to further my education so I took my college boards and, I applied for _____ [university]. I was accepted but after 2 semesters, I decided "the hell with it" and I stopped going to school and began working full time. Working became a drag after a while and I didn't know what to do until I had a fight with my boss until I quit. I started collecting unemployment. I loafed and I had a great time doing nothing. Eventually unemployment ran out and I went back to work at the bicycle shop where I am still working. I decided to try school again. Not being able to attend the.school that I wanted to go to first, City Community College was recommended so I applied. So now I am back in school hoping it would give me some idea of what I will do in the future. Things are unorganized, but enjoyable here and I am hoping that I will establish a foundation for which I can go on to better things.

(from a student's essay)

I didn't want to go to school and didn't ever bother to apply myself. I never made it to high school classes and by graduation time I was failing 2 majors. I got my diploma and was feeling pretty guilty for I didn't think I really deserved it. . . . Around April I had gone into a depression where nothing interested me. After graduation my boyfriend seemed to lose interest in me and I delayed his leaving for a while, 'til I was sure I couldn't keep him happy anymore. . . . At the same time I saw an ad for this school. I decided to apply for February admission but found out there was room in September classes. So here I am.

I hope this is what I need to get me off on the right path in life and to give me time to mature a little before I go off on my own. . . . I haven't decided or thought much about what I will use my education for, for I think it will fall into place when the time comes.

(from a student's essay)

I wanted to come back to school because I had to. I did shit in high school and you guys know about my job history. [Laughter] I had eight god-damn jobs in two years. What a fuck-off!

(in conversation with four students)

Do you want to know the real reason I'm here? Because I'm a dunce. I got lost in junior high school. If I was smart I wouldn't be here, I'd be at _____ College [a nearby four-year college] and be on my way to becoming something.

(in conversation with a student)

Stewart: So she [the admissions officer] asks me why I want to come here. I told her, "To get a position like yours." She'd know that if she was a flunky.

(from an overheard conversation)

I sit [in the school cafeteria] with a group of fire science students who are complaining about the chemistry test, how poorly they did and how hard it was. They say it is much harder than an introductory course should be.

Jack (satirically): "You don't see Bill here worrying, do you? He knows he's all washed up." Laughter. "You don't see me worrying either. So I get an F—big deal."

Bill: "I know'd I should of stayed in high school." He laughs alone, a long self-pitying laugh.

Jack: "Christ, if I'd of stayed back last year like they told me I wouldn't be stuck now." More self-pitying laughter.

(lunchtime conversation)

In school, because I devoted the majority of my time towards sports, my academic education was below average. I won all kinds of athletic awards, but I was the class dunce. "All muscle and no brain" they use to say about me.

(from a student's essay)

Rose and Donna are discussing Rose's math course. At one point Rose said that the course was very difficult for almost everybody even though most had covered the material in high school.

Donna: "Ya, I know I flunked algebra twice."

Rose: "We ought to be taking basic math [course title]. I heard they're just doing fractions."

Donna: "I *am* taking basic math and that's what we're doing."

Rose: "Really?"

Donna: "It's like seventh grade. Like it's good because you go back over it all, but you feel kind of stupid, you know what I mean?"

(from an overheard conversation)

Oftentimes students more explicitly compared themselves to senior college students or to middle-class people in general. Although comparing themselves unfavorably in terms of academic capacities and intelligence, they often resented the snobbery and condescension of the reference group:

Dave told me that while in high school he worked nights in a restaurant washing dishes, doing chores, and general cleaning. He claims he became night manager. After graduating high school and avoiding the draft with a high lottery number, he worked in a shoe store for one year. "It was dumb, a real nothin' job." He went to another community college for one semester but dropped out because of a low average and because most of the students were from _____, ____ ____, and _____ [affluent suburbs]: "Snotty as hell," he says of them. "You know, they thought they were at Harvard or MIT."

(conversation in a bar)

Al: "Hey, I got an A on my report."

Sean: "Yeah? So you want a star on your forehead?"

Al: "Oh, man, it was great, he thought I was smart, like I was from _____ [an affluent suburb]."

Tom: "Yeah, or maybe _____ or _____ [two more affluent suburbs]." They all smile at this as we enter the classroom together.

(hallway conversation)

Teacher: "Do you think people in the upper classes read more?"

Joan: "Oh sure, they have more free time."

Leo: "Upper-class people aren't able to enjoy themselves as much as lower-class people. I'd rather be out enjoying myself than reading books. How many rich kids know what it's like to hang out in a group? Lower-class people maybe don't learn much about books, but we learn a lot about people."

Mike: "One difference is that they don't ask for ice cream for dessert. They ask for yogurt or a piece of celery." [Laughter]

Sal: "They just built a new library here in _____ [section of the city], right? The people were bullshit. We don't even have a good movie theater. Now how many people do you really think are going to use it? This ain't _____ [an affluent suburb]."

(a social science class)

During her talk Jane said, "This [City Community College] isn't like high school." This was met by a chorus of "no's" and guffaws. I missed exactly what was said—there were a number of simultaneous conversations, but I did hear Alice say, "The students here are bitter." After the meeting ended I asked what she meant. She told me that a lot of the liberal arts students were not admitted to "regular schools" and that City Community College was their last choice. "It all started in high school. Their friends got into _____ College [a four-year school] or somewhere and they ask, 'Where are you going?' Then you say 'City Community College.' You know—no one's ever heard of it. And besides it's a *community* college [her emphasis] in _____ [name of the larger city, in which there are several eminent universities]. So forget it. It can't be college." She adds that she has heard it will be difficult to transfer to a good college. She thinks the attitudes of outsiders to the community college are "closed-minded" and that the comparisons are a "put-down."

(conversation after a student government meeting)

Ray: "There are schools and there are colleges."

HBL: "What do you mean?"

Ray: "This isn't a *college* college. It just seems more like a high school. It's a feeling I have. It's not just because I commute, because I have friends who commute to _____ College and they don't think that it's like high school."

(conversation in the student cafeteria)

Pam: "For a lot of kids this school is the joke of the year." Jean agrees.

I ask what they mean.

Pam: "They admitted everyone who applied, didn't they? They

really had to, it being a new school. My friends who go to _____
and _____ [two state colleges]. They all think it's a joke because
anyone could get in. Jean, you know Barbara Doyle, right? She comes
home from school Thanksgiving and says, 'Well, how's City Community College?' real bitchy like." Jean says she never liked Barbara.

(conversation in the student lounge)

As the following comments illustrate, the students' self-doubts led
them to appreciate they had arrived at a critical and fateful juncture in
their lives:

Nothing but disappointment has been my past experience so City
Community College is my last hope.

(from a student's essay)

My mother taught me how to be a lady and a housewife. My father,
because I was a girl, always referred me to my mother when times
of crisis would arrive. His most famous saying was, "Never work in
a factory. Get an education, so you can go to work clean and come
home the same way." It didn't make much sense to me when I was
young but as I got older I began to understand.

(from a student's essay)

I quit public high school and joined the U.S. Navy.... I also completed high school while in the service. My return to civilian life was
somewhat a shocking experience. In the Navy, I had not truly considered my future life, and now I was face-to-face with the responsibility
of choosing my future life-freedom. After working several odd jobs,
I entered a community college in _____ [another city]. Surpris-
ingly, I managed average grades, the first quarter, but I withdrew
from the second quarter. I worked for _____, didn't like it and quit.
Now I am determined to stay in school. I can't afford not to.

(from a student's essay)

My eventual goal is to major in Phys. Ed. and History. I hope my
teachers will feel free to give me advice and assistance at every
opportunity. I need all the help I can get. It has been a long time since
the last time I have applied myself.

(from a student's essay)

Steve told me that he was rejected at two colleges but put on the
waiting list at two others, both state colleges. He applied to City
Community College in late August and was notified of his acceptance
three days later. After this last information he immediately says,
"Wow! I figured maybe I better not go there. If they took me that fast
they're probably getting the bottom of the high school classes. But I
knew if I went out working for six months it would be balls to get
back in."

(conversation in the student lounge)

Tom: "I was at U_____ [the state university] last year but only lasted one semester. I didn't like it there—it was too impersonal and the classes were too big. I better like it here." I ask what he means by his last remark and he tells me that if he doesn't make it through City Community College he will have to find a job in a very depressed labor market.

(conversation in the library)

Don: "I graduated high school eight and a half years ago, went into the service, and worked at all kinds of jobs. What the hell do I have to show for it? A decent car, that's all. If I don't get my ass in gear I might not even have that."

(conversation in the cafeteria)

John told me he worked for the telephone company for a year after he was discharged from the Marines. He didn't like the work very much: "There was nothing in it. Who wants to fix telephones every day?" He was planning to attend _____ State but thought there were too many required courses. He walked out halfway through the registration process: "My wife gave me hell for a year, so when this place opened, I came here." He is majoring in human services. "I knew it was time to make a break. If I waited any longer it would be too late."

(conversation while waiting for a class)

In the face of their concerns and self-doubts, it would be logical to expect students to work hard in school in order to "reestablish" themselves. After all, they were in school not despite their anxieties but because of them. Yet they did not "seize the hour". In class after class it was painfully obvious that reading and writing assignments were often undone, that students were unwilling to engage in class discussions, and that attendance was poor. Observations such as the following were common:

Franklin [the teacher] begins the class by saying that for the last week they have been discussing _____ [title of a book]. "Has everyone read it?" There is no response from the students. He asks: "OK, how many have read the book?" Six people raise their hands—one third of the class.

Franklin: "Well, that's not bad—even if it has been over one week." He begins discussing the book.

(a social science class)

She [the teacher] circulates the weekly attendance sheet. When it comes to me I see that out of a class of 25, 16 were present on Monday, 13 on Tuesday, and 8 on Wednesday.

(an English class)

The kinds of questions asked of the students can be answered in one sentence, but there are no volunteers and she must call on the students.

(a biology class)

At one point he [the teacher] says, "You did read the article, didn't you?" Three say they have, the others just sit. Marshall says softly, but loud enough for all to hear, "I thought there was some confusion."

(a social science class)

Teacher: "I had them read _____ [book title] and I told them we were going to discuss it on a certain day and on that day hardly anybody showed up. That was no coincidence."

(a social science teacher)

The class was to read _____ [book title]. Jones begins by explaining that each student must decide today on which of the book's concepts they will write their essays. He asks if any have already decided. There is no response. He asks how many have read the book. Four students (out of 32) raise their hands.

(a social science class)

Once Stickland [the teacher] has gone off on a tangent in response to George's question, the others keep asking him questions about it. They stay on this topic until the bell rings. As I leave the room with George and Ray, Ray says, "Hey, that was OK. Who's going to ask a question tomorrow? You do it, Tom."

Tom says he will think of one. He adds, "We had him going for almost the whole hour today." They congratulate each other on diverting the teacher from the book they had to discuss.

(a social science class)

Jones [the teacher] has difficulty getting students to respond. He walks to the back of the room and calls on two students seated there —no response. A third student volunteers at last.

(a business class)

She [the teacher] asks who has written the assignment. Only one has [out of 12]. She asks them to write it now. No visible signs of anger. Then she states: "I know that only one person has read chapters one and two. I just want to remind you that when you take out a reserve book you have to sign your name."

(a music class)

She [the teacher] asks if there are any questions. Silence.
Teacher: "The class is getting that morguelike quality again!"

(a social science class)

Logan [the teacher] asks for the students' evaluations of the case, how they think a judge might decide. No one volunteers.

Logan: "Don't be afraid. How about you, Mr. Walsh?"

Walsh: "What do you want me to do?"

Lagan reexplains. Walsh offers a short answer. Logan asks for other comments, but no one volunteers.

(a law enforcement class)

He [the teacher] asks how many have actually read the book assigned. Twelve students (out of 24) raise their hands.

Teacher: "Well, that's better than in the other class. Only five people read it. We've been talking about the book for five weeks now and in the other class they all go, 'Ya, ya,' and nod their heads when I talk about the book. Then I found out only five people read it. Some of them told me they read the first chapter and maybe the second and thought they could figure out the rest." Laughter from the class. "I guess I'm lucky here—half of you people read it."

(a social science class)

They turn to today's lesson concerning the movie *Love Story.* Cunningham asks, "Who wants to give a synopsis of the movie?" No response.

Cunningham: "Come on! This whole semester you've been so nonverbal! Terry, you do it."

Terry: "No, you."

Cunningham: "I'm not going to do all the work."

Terry: "OK." She then gives a very short summary—three or four sentences. The class responds very little, or not at all, to further questions and Cunningham winds up giving the synopsis. Next they are to discuss an article they were assigned, but only two students have read it. Cunningham ends by saying: "For tomorrow, my unworking little chickadees, I want you to outline the article and the author's main arguments."

(an English class)

While the level of effort could not be objectively documented, attendance could.* During the first three weeks of school, attendance

---

*Because the school consisted of one large building, it was possible to count the number of students by peering through the windowpanes of class doors and by walking through the corridors and lounges. Head counts were made two or three times per week during morning classes; while all students had morning classes, on some days some students did not have afternoon classes. It was necessary to begin the count at the beginning of an hour to complete it before the classes moved to different rooms. While counting I would walk the corridors nonchalantly eating a sandwich, sipping coffee, or, if in a crowded lounge or in the cafeteria, feign searching for someone. While so scanning I would count.

averaged from 850 to 950 (out of 1,103). For the remainder of the year (excluding exam periods) the average head count was 525 (with a range from 192 to 852). Although the margin of error is unknown, the 525 average means that on a typical day more than half the student body was absent. The first edition of the student newspaper, published only eight weeks after the start of classes, featured an editorial on absenteeism, the lead sentence reading: "Believe it or not, a college student has certain recognizable responsibilities. The major responsibility is to actually attend college."

The preceding data suggest that in City Community College, students created a perspective that diminished the possibility of success as defined by their middle-class, gate-keeping teachers. Indeed, the self-doubts of students, so intimately linked with social class, created a double bind: Suspecting their abilities to work with ideas led them to suspect the worth of working with ideas, yet mind and intelligence were held to be important indicators of worth and character.[14] The students' problem, then, was to define an unfamiliar institution, an institution that, on the one hand, might be the vehicle for a critical opportunity, but, on the other hand, might injure them further. It is no coincidence that the Chinese brush strokes that represent opportunity stand also for danger. To understand more fully how students managed this dilemma, it is first necessary to examine the expectations, values, and career paths of their teachers.

NOTES

1. U.S. Bureau of the Census, *1970 Census of Population and Housing* (Washington, D.C.: U.S. Government Printing Office, 1970).

2. W.S. Robinson, "Ecological Correlations and the Behavior of Individuals," *American Sociological Review* 15 (June 1950): 351–57.

3. Peter Binzen, *Whitetown, U.S.A.* (New York: Random House, 1970), pp. 3–4.

4. Similar leisure-time activities (or lack of them) are described in Diana Wolman, "The Unknown Student: Notes from a New England Community College," unpublished paper, Department of Sociology, University of Massachusetts at Boston, 1973.

5. K. Patricia Cross, *The Junior College Students: A Research Description* (Princeton, N.J.: Educational Testing Service, 1968), p. 32.

6. K. Patricia Cross, *Beyond the Open Door: New Students to Higher Education* (San Francisco: Jossey-Bass, 1971), pp. 13–14.

7. Lewis Anthony Dexter, *The Tyranny of Schooling* (New York: Basic Books, 1964), p. 20.

8. William Ryan, *Blaming the Victim* (New York: Random House, 1971), p. 4.

9. Ibid., pp. 30–35.

10. This sense of honor is what Max Weber refers to as status honor. This is discussed throughout in Chapters 3 and 4. See Guenther Ross and Claus Wittich, eds., *Max Weber: Economy and Society* (New York: Bedminster Press, 1968), vol. 2, pp. 932–33.

11. Elliot Liebow, *Tally's Corner: A Study of Negro Streetcorner Men* (Boston: Little, Brown, 1967), p. 222.

12. Herbert H. Hyman, "The Value Systems of Different Classes: A Social Psychological Contribution to the Analysis of Stratification," in *Class, Status and Power: A Reader in Social Stratification,* ed. Reinhard Bendix and Seymour M. Lipset (Glencoe, Ill.: Free Press, 1966), p. 498.

13. The concept of "comparative failure" is adapted from Robert R. Faulkner, *Hollywood Studio Musicians: Their Work and Careers in the Recording Industry* (Chicago: Aldine/Atherton, 1971), pp. 52–53; and Lawrence Chenowith, *The American Dream of Success: The Search for the Self in the Twentieth Century* (Belmont, Calif: Wadsworth, 1974), pp. 165–78.

14. For a complete discussion of the relationship between self-assessments of intelligence and self-worth among working-class people, see Richard Sennett and Jonathan Cobb, *The Hidden Injuries of Class* (New York: Random House, 1972).

2
THE TEACHERS: CAREER PATH AND IDENTITY

The folly of that impossible precept, "Know thyself"; till it be translated into this partially possible one, "Know what thou canst work at."
—Thomas Carlyle

To study careers is to study identities.[1] As stated by Everett
Hughes, who pioneered the sociological study of careers and occupations:

> The career includes not only the processes and sequences of learning
> the techniques of the occupation but also the progressive perception
> of the whole system and of possible places in it and the accompanying
> changes in conceptions of the work and of one's self in relation to it.[2]

More specifically, as a person's career unfolds, changes in social position
are intertwined with changes in adult identity. In their analysis of
adult socialization, Howard Becker and Anselm Strauss conclude that
as people's careers

> carry them up, along and down, to unexpected places and to novel
> experiences even when in some sense foreseen, [they] must gain,
> maintain and regain a sense of personal identity. Identity "is never
> gained nor maintained once and for all."[3]

The career path of community college teachers in the United
States, and certainly at City Community College, is as yet uninstitution-
alized. Despite the lack of a formalized career path, there are notable
similarities in the unexpected places and novel experiences to which
community college teachers have been taken, as well as in the self-
redefinitions these journeys have prompted.[4] The purpose of this chapter is to trace the career paths of CCC teachers and to relate these paths
to identities and perspectives. The data are derived from classroom

observation, informal conversations outside the class, and in-depth tape-recorded interviews of 37 of the 53 instructors (70 percent).

The similarities in their careers are found in the convergence of events and circumstances that required the making of fateful career decisions. Some contingencies were personal, such as family concerns; some were organizational, such as bureaucratic reorganizations; and some were cultural and historical, such as a shifting political and ideological climate. However, in each case the meeting of contingencies was critical in terms of career direction and in strengthening or weakening loyalty and commitment to an organizational setting and occupational gestalt.

Let us first consider the liberal arts and human services teachers and then the vocational faculty. (Liberal arts teachers also taught the human services courses; see discussion further on.)

Of the 28 (of 40) liberal arts-human services teachers interviewed, 22 shared a critical career experience: Their expectations of teaching in a four-year college or university had to be changed after having taken at least the initial steps toward a Ph.D. These were not vague expectations but well-defined career plans that were upset. Table 2.1 shows that of the five teachers with only a bachelor's degree, four had altered career paths. Of the 21 master's degree teachers interviewed, 16 had either withdrawn from doctoral programs, been denied admission, or been prevented from applying for financial and family reasons (to be discussed). Four of the 21 were still enrolled in Ph.D. tracts. The two Ph.D.s interviewed had searched unsuccessfully for university positions.

TABLE 2.1: Degrees and Expectations of Liberal Arts and Human Services Instructors

Highest Degree Earned	Number of Teachers	Number Interviewed	Senior College Teaching Expectations
B.A.	5	5	4
M.A.	32	21	16
Ph.D.	3	2	2
Total	40	28	22

Source: U.S. Bureau of the Census, 1970.

One set of contingencies responsible for the career twist was biological age, coupled with the press of personal, family, and economic burdens. The following are descriptions of these contingencies from recorded interviews:*

After I got married I had no further educational background [beyond the bachelor's degree]. There was a period when I went part time to _____ University in _____ [subject matter] for about two years and actually finished work for a doctoral thesis, but I was just busy what with being employed full time and with my family that I never finished my course work. . . . I maybe had out of 16 courses four or five of them. My work corresponded with what could have been used for a thesis . . . that's how I got my data. . . . Athletically I was competing seriously at a national level in track. Meanwhile I was also having children, which meant that something had to go, and what went was the attempt to go in science. If you don't get a doctorate you can't plan to go on and this was the reason that decision had to be made. I could not raise a family, continue in sports, get a doctorate, and in the sports you couldn't prolong this either. Getting a doctorate in science at an older age just doesn't work as opposed to other fields. It's just uncommon. If you are going to do significant work it's at a younger age. In sports you can't prolong the aging process, so there was the decision. If it had been in English, I might have been able to go on and do it.

Right after I got my M.A. I naturally wanted to get a job in _____ [home state]. We had a real nice home there. Both our families [his and his wife's] live there and I thought that's what I'd like to do, but the job market kept getting tighter and tighter. I applied to the local four-year colleges but they didn't like my qualifications; they wanted a doctorate. I started taking some courses for my doctorate but just then my wife became pregnant. I would still like to end up working for a doctorate, but [when I found out about teaching in the community college] I just had to take it. It was an offer I couldn't refuse.

By the time I finished college I was pretty much oriented toward a career in college teaching. I had a commission in the service through ROTC and after two years returned to the University of _____. I did all the course work for the doctorate in _____ [subject matter]. I never took exams and didn't write the dissertation. There was a possibility of teaching in a community college and four-year college positions were *extremely* difficult to find. That would have to be

---

*Because this chapter contains much personal information teachers cannot be identified by academic area or age. The space between excerpts signifies a different interview.

mentioned very, very quickly as one reason for discontinuing my doctoral studies.

Right at the time when I finished my master's certainly I wanted a career but I was open-minded in that as a woman, more so at that time, one had to figure, yes, you wanted to have a career and you would let it evolve in a focused way as much as possible in a way consistent with what your husband did. [After taking some doctoral courses I realized] it had to be consistent with what my husband and children were doing. But it wasn't. When I was divorced 10 years ago I didn't have the resources to go back to graduate school.

I was doing graduate work at the beginning of the semester for a combination master's-doctorate, but I canceled out because I couldn't handle the load they were giving me and then developing the program here too. . . . Last summer I rationalized I needed the job. I was married, owned a home and was supporting my in-laws.

I just assumed that I would get a B.A. degree, get a master's degree, get a Ph.D. and teach in a university. It seemed that simple until I got out into the real world and realized what it was really like. . . . Had I not been accepted here I suppose I would have finished the master's and gone for a Ph.D. . . . But I did get this job, so now the idea of a Ph.D., knowing what that's worth today with the competition, I just feel that if you get a job, that's far more important—holding onto the job—than another diploma. A job came along and that was more important.

I was nine hours into the doctoral program when it just struck me as silly. I mean the market was glutted with _____ [subject matter] Ph.D.s. Economically, it wasn't worth that much investment.

And the reason for that [discontinuing her doctoral studies] is because of general personal life—moving into a new home, an old home that had to be renovated, and then I had my little one last year, which means that constitutes not having the time for work, family life, and going to school.

At the time I was applying for jobs I was restricting myself to this area for family reasons primarily. I applied mostly to four-year schools like _____ and _____. I received an offer from City Community but didn't pick up on it. During the year and a half or so that followed, I began to think this was my last chance since the work situation was so bad.

I applied to _____ for my doctorate because it's supposed to have a good radical _____ department. But then I got this wonderful letter from the University of _____ saying there were all these people interested in all these things I'm interested in. And I said, "Well, I'll go there," and I was very, very disappointed in the program and the students. I thought they were all very rhetorical and just spouting Marxism without thinking it through.

But I graduated in 1953 with Phi Beta Kappa, magna cum laude with distinction in _____ [subject matter]. In the fall of '53 I started at _____ as a teaching assistant and Ph.D. candidate in _____. A year later ... or two years later the teaching assistantship was changed to half time instructor but I was still a Ph.D. candidate and during this time I was still working part time at the _____ Research Center.

Interviewer: Did you get a master's degree?

Teacher: No, I went in the program which bypassed that.... In fact I have only the bachelor's degree now. I never picked up the master's. In the spring of 1958 I got an unsolicited phone call which essentially changed my life. It was from the present of _____ Community College, which hadn't yet started, and he was soliciting a staff and had heard of me as a teacher through his connection in _____ [name of city]. I still don't know how he singled me out. In September of 1958 I started as one of the six original faculty members together with 100 students and formed _____ Community College. And I remained there for just 10 years, exactly 10 years.

Interviewer: Did you drop your doctoral candidacy?

Teacher: Yes. In fact I went up there for one year as an experiment. What really happened was just an interesting circumstance. My thesis adviser had a Guggenheim Fellowship to be in Oxford, England, at the same time ... for the year in which the President of _____ [the community college] had asked me to come down. And I felt I wasn't taking a chance at all because I felt it was as easy to write to my adviser as long as he was going to be in England. I could just as easily write from _____ Community College as from _____ University. The part that was interesting that I overlooked and probably also changed my life was that the university atmosphere wasn't there. In other words there was nobody there to encourage me to do my _____ research.... I actually reached the stage where I had written one thesis that had been rejected because the results had been too negative. In fact I am not that sure but that if I had been in a lesser institution that the thesis wouldn't have been accepted. I think it was a combination of two things: one was that it was _____ University where a lot was expected of you and the other was that my thesis adviser felt that I was much more intelligent in _____ [subject matter] than I really think that I am. But I actually reached the stage where every requirement for the Ph.D. had been fulfilled except for the thesis and even there I had written one. It was going to be sharpened. Of course what happened in the 10 years at _____ Community College I drifted away from [pause].... The

frontiers of theoretical _____ are such that if you stay away from
it for a while it's like you've never been there. It's like learning to
type, but then never touching a typewriter. So actually I'm further
away from [pause] . . . it sounds funny but I'm further away from a
Ph.D. right now than I was 15 years ago.

Other teachers withdrew because they were unsure of their interests or their competence:

I discontinued because I just wasn't mature enough to handle Ph.D.
work, I thought at the time. It wasn't so difficult academically, but I
didn't feel I was synthesizing well and knew the directions I wanted
to go in.

Up to that time I enjoyed scientific research and I was working on my
master's degree and enjoyed it thoroughly. It was a fun game, but
there I just felt that probably I had more to offer in education than
I could as an individual offer in research, because at that time I
realized I'm no Charles Darwin. I would have been a second-rate
researcher.

Four other liberal arts teachers left nonacademic careers to enroll
in graduate school in the hope of becoming university professors. They
started too late:

From 1940 I worked for 30 years and 6 months as a _____ [low skill
job]. . . . And in 1960 I graduated at 56 years of age with all the kids.
After getting my master's degree at _____ College, I really, seriously, thought about getting a Ph.D. and teaching in a [four-year]
college myself. Let me put it frankly, I didn't only for one reason—
I think you have to be realistic about your age. I don't feel old, but
I'm almost 62, and I already made one big change in my life. You
know, we try to teach our students to be motivated and yet realistic
—and we have to be the same ourselves.

My wife and I typed every one of 500 letters. We did it in a regional
way. I set out first to teach in one of the _____ [geographic region]
colleges, because I'm from [that area]. And then our next choice was
the New England area and we blanketed the New England area. My
original intent was to apply to four-year colleges, but by the time
you're writing 500 letters it doesn't make any difference. . . . The point
that several people made known to me right away or as soon as I was
seriously job hunting was the fact that at 50 you cannot go to a
graduate school, that the graduate schools were hiring assistants and
instructors in their old 20s who had that book behind them, and that
they were not that interested in a 50-year-old unless that 50-year-old
could some way or another convert his dissertation into a Pulitzer

Prize. And thus the idea was that no matter what I wanted to do I would very probably never be able to apply to a graduate school—a university.

The two Ph.D.s interviewed came to CCC after adverse experiences in four-year institutions; family concerns also played a part. Reported one:

I taught there [a university] for three years 'til I began to have the problem of tenure and rehiring and what not. It was at that point that I had to make a decision and because of my experience and general education, I took a job at the _____ [a school for medical paraprofessionals] to help develop a social science program.

Interviewer: I missed it. Why did you leave _____ University?

Teacher: You mean why wasn't I kept? There was a change in administration and the head of our department, who said as long as he'd be there, I'd be there, retired. There was a new dean of the college and we didn't get along very well. . . . It was full time, it was a *good* job. . . . Now I only stayed one year there; I was happy there, things were going very well, but an old friend of mine was made president of _____ College and it was at *that* point that I had to make a very critical life decision; that is, do I want to stay with the professional school giving special kinds of courses or do I want to go back to a traditional general ed program that I left at _____ University and always felt a little sad about leaving. So I picked the decision of going to [the college at which his friend was made president]. . . . But I soon found it was not really for me. [He discusses three reasons: his family's unhappiness in an isolated midwestern town, the overly traditional and locally oriented faculty, and the college's financial difficulties.] I tried to get my old job back but of course it was gone. We wanted so much to come back to this area. I began earnestly looking about January. We had a break—I saw an article about City Community College and made an appointment with the new president. And I began to pursue that seriously. I checked out _____ Community College, checked out other community colleges, state schools. I tried all my contacts. It was very tight. I tried everything. Four-year schools. . . . See by this time of course the disaster hit this area in terms of jobs and openings.

Interviewer: At that particular time, would you rather have taught in a community college or a four-year school?

Teacher: It's really hard to know in a way because of course the panic of getting a job, any job. . . . Of course you're asking this at a bad time, after living four places and having three jobs within the last couple of years. There was the psychological factor of moving and dislocating and we were already settled in this area. . . . And with the two kids and everything, you know, I never thought about security, but there is that element now. It creeps into it.

Liberal arts and human services teachers are considered together in this chapter not only because of their common career aspirations and career paths but because most taught students in both programs; furthermore, their classes were more intellectually oriented than the vocational courses. "Intellectually oriented" does not mean they taught highly advanced courses, but that in contrast to the vocational programs requiring rote memorization and the acquisition of physical skills, their courses required students to manipulate and synthesize abstract ideas and concepts. As the following representative comments indicate, these teachers retained a strong belief in the independent worth and efficacy of working with ideas and abstractions; in this fundamental sense, they were confirmed intellectuals.

> The way a college originally evolved—the English and European universities—was for the intellectuals and this pattern in a sense has been copied to apply to everybody. Now this doesn't make sense to my way of thinking. . . . It seems to me there ought to be other forms [of education] in our lives today. . . . I think that what I really feel is you shouldn't have students taking a _____ [the teacher's subject matter] course or certain other types of courses who aren't intellectually going to be scholars. In other words, college is designed basically for scholars, and either change the college or don't admit a lot of students. Now I think at a community college they are essentially trying to have courses that are appropriate but you are still running into the liberal arts students who want to transfer. I expect the number of students who are getting through to four-year colleges is out of proportion, for you know that they don't all become scholars.

> The students in our courses—they're doing it largely because they've got to pass the course. They really don't reach the point of finding it intellectually interesting to know why something happens. They know they have to learn it for whatever reason, but they don't often find "isn't that interesting" as a separate issue in itself.

> When I first started out [as a student] I'm not sure I achieved in college for the sheer love of achievement. I worked because of grades. And then once I started I found the process interesting enough so that learning became important to me for itself. I mean nothing in my background had made me want to learn for the sheer joy and sake of learning as I've come to appreciate.

> Even in a vocational program I think if we are *pretending* [teacher's emphasis] that we are giving something like two years of college then we're obligated to give them an academic component and that means

working with ideas. Now if a student really finds that so alien to them that they don't want to have anything to do with it, then sometimes I advise them to think about what they are doing and whether this is really the best place for them.

It was at that part [in the teacher's career] that I really found the *right* kind of teaching [his emphasis].

Interviewer: Can you describe what you mean by that?

Teacher: Ya, well, the program at _____ University was the program for liberal arts students who had picked the program themselves and had to be in the upper half of their class.... It was a high-geared academic thing, derivative of the old University of Chicago program, the Hutchinson program. And in that program I taught with people of other disciplines and I taught interdisciplinary stuff—which is always what I've wanted to do. So it was the *ideal* teaching situation for a person with my background. Although my degrees were in _____, my interests were broader than that. And here was a chance to do *all* of the social sciences. It was very exciting, stimulating.

I'm turned on when in class I have people who ask me questions which come out of their own independent reflection, out of their own musing, out of their own inquisitiveness. That makes a whole section for me. If I have two or three people like that in a section—wow!—it's a pleasure.

You know, a student might be a crackerjack carpenter or mechanic, or somebody who has great insight into putting things together, which requires a level of intelligence which is impressive, but my own inclination, since the kinds of courses I teach don't deal with those kinds of mechanical skills, is to try to help them make contact with an idea. And I'll do anything that I can to introduce them to this kind of a world.

I don't think my background was as impoverished intellectually as I feel some of these kids are, because I did grow up in an atmosphere that was certainly concerned with ideas. My mother's favorite fellow was Walter Lippmann. We were concerned with ideas. I can sympathize with these kids because I know that that's not so for them.

I think that the kids are alienated from working with ideas that seemingly have no relationship to their lives. The ideas that I try to communicate and have them get excited about are ideas that I think are real pertinent to their lives.

Those teachers with previous nonacademic occupations were quick to point out that they had been intellectually alive long before returning to school:

I *must* point out, because I think it would be deceptive if I didn't, that I've always been a reader. It isn't as if I went to school without any notion at all about how to pick up a book and read it. I read all my life and, you know, read fairly good stuff—classics, that kind of thing. But, anyway, I took that one course [in a nearby university] and became intrigued by the whole notion and got into the program by the next year in a more disciplined way. . . .

Somewhere along the line—in my middle thirties—I *finally* decided I was really missing out on things and I started going to night school.

  Interviewer: What do you mean by "missing out on things"?

  Teacher: Just intellectually . . . there were things happening that I just wasn't aware of, that I didn't understand. There were words on the radio or things in the newspapers, concepts that I knew existed but didn't understand. And I started back to night school.

So I got out of high school—graduated on a Wednesday, I'll never forget it—and I started working on Thursday morning after I had been salutatorian in high school and something of a big fish in a little pond. Suddenly on Thursday I found myself working for four lawyers who referred to me as "the girl," which, you know, offended my highly developed sense of person even then. I knew though that I wanted to go to school, it was just that there was never any question that I would have to go to work to support myself and my mother. It was extremely difficult for me. I worked there for five years until I decided I *had* to go to school and I went to _____ College—it was the commercial arm of _____ University. I remember standing in line waiting to register for what I thought would be a commercial career in college. I remember the building on _____ Street and _____ Avenue. It's still there; it was a tall office building—commercial building. And while I was standing in line I decided that this is not what I wanted; I didn't want the commercial life. I knew I couldn't stand it. I just got out of line and came home. I decided then that I would go to an academic college, which I did. Throughout all this time I worked full time for these four men. It took me nine and a half years to get the degree. I was not going to be unhappy because my own sense of self-image had to be submerged. I graduated *Phi Beta Kappa.*

The internalization of intellectual values commits a person to a self-concept. Howard Becker has stated:

> commitments are not necessarily made consciously and deliberately. Some commitments do result from conscious decisions, but others arise crescively; the person becomes aware that he is committed only at some point of change and seems to have made the commitment without realizing it.[5]

Regardless of the contingencies that ended their graduate careers or, in the case of the Ph.D.s, their university careers, teaching in the community college was seen as a way to maintain both the intellectual commitment and the accompanying self-image, although (as discussed below) in modified form. As Becker suggests, however, it was during the various career turning points that many of the teachers became quite anxious about the potential inability to act upon their commitments, as that directly threatened their very identities. In a word, these people were disappointed. For some the fracture between expectations and reality was severe:

> You can't study for a doctorate in a real good school without wanting to deal with it at a high level. I think that the whole excitement of _____ [academic area], of the seminars, and the detail work of the graduate school is such that your first choice would be to have a seminar of your own. . . . It requires a definite step to turn your back on a dissertation that you *ate* and *dreamt* and *breathed* and *slept* for three or four years. It took me that long to get my dissertation in the shape that it's in. And the simple truth is, you turn your back on that and you almost don't even refer to it in this whole period of time [since coming to City Community College]. Now I think that the commitment that it takes to write a dissertation is a commitment that is difficult to turn your back on. It is disappointing. I'll say it's difficult to make that kind of decision, because you turn your back on something that you've committed five years of your life to.

> Anyway, after I was rejected for the Ph.D. candidacy there was a _____ [academic area] convention in the city, so I went looking for a job, and I was looking either for a research or teaching job in _____ [academic area]. I would have taken any kind of job I was so uptight.

For others the disappointment seemed less intense:

> It was upsetting when I left the chairman's office the day I withdrew [from the graduate program]. I went in with such high hopes. At any rate, I scoured the city until I found this [job]. I was anxious, but determined.

The two Ph.D.s would rather have taken positions in four-year colleges. Said one who was unsuccessful in finding such a job:

> If [the job offer] had been a four-year state school such as University of _____, I mean I wouldn't care what the name of it was, _____ State, anything! If it was something I knew was as substantial and had the "let-me-alone" principle at work, I probably would have taken the four-year [school].

These teachers, like their students, felt that somewhere along the line an opportunity was missed or that somehow they had not performed as they wished they had. Yet, however intense their career disappointment and however willingly or unwillingly they acknowledged it, the teachers clearly redefined both self and career in order to deflect, minimize, or rationalize that disappointment. In their attempted redefinitions, they infused their new role with values (discussed below) previously unappreciated. In short, to the extent that work is an indication of self-worth, the unplanned-for move became a virtuous move.

The intent in the following analysis of this phenomenon is not to debunk community college teachers, but to show how, as do people in other occupations, they cushion themselves against the precariousness, strains, and tensions of their careers.[6] Considered first is the content of the redefinitions; second, the social process through which the redefinitions were transmitted and enforced; and third, the relationship between the redefinitions and the structure of higher education.

The chief self- and career redefinition involved the devaluing of research and scholarly activity and the emphasizing of quality, humanistic teaching:[7]

> I had always wanted to go into medicine or medical research; I even did get into research for a while but without the doctorate this was going to be useless. . . . [Later in the interview] Part of the reason I'm teaching here is that I knew that I wanted to do it to expand my experience. As far as anything else goes I have a basic interest in learning and growing myself, which is sort of inherent. You've got to have that or you are going to be helpless in teaching. There is a great deal more for me to learn as far as teaching in the community college. I know I need another couple of years to have a better feel and have more success in teaching.

> I thought about doing some research work in _____ and _____ [subject areas]. . . . I feel as if I'm more than adequately qualified to teach and I don't really have a lot of anticipations of doing a lot of publication work. It's less important to me now.

> _____ College was an experimental college. While I was teaching there [with doctoral course work in progress] I spent a great deal of time discussing the nature of the freshman _____ [subject area] class and we had several good professors and got a lot of different opinions as to what should be taught. I became very interested in this. I think it was probably then I decided to go into junior college teaching and made a conscious decision to go into junior colleges because up to that point I had been considering getting my Ph.D. and going into university teaching . . .

Interviewer: Why junior college as opposed to teaching in a university or four-year college?

Teacher: Because I was more interested in educational aspects than I was in the research. I feel that the purpose of the university is towards research and more important than the actual teaching. You could actually have the university without having any students, as far as I'm concerned, because that's the importance of a university, but I was more interested in the educational aspects than I was in the research. . . . I really wasn't interested in research and of course that's what a Ph.D. does.

I don't see that I would want to move on to a four-year college to teach at a four-year college. . . . I'm not that kind of a scholar, you know, I don't want to become a scholar. To teach at a really good university you really need some, some esoteric specialty that you know backwards and forwards and that you've researched and I don't think that's what life is about and I don't think that that's what I want to teach about. I think if I were to perform the perfect act for each of my students, it wouldn't be to have them read any research I might do, but to teach them how to ask questions, not what the wisdom of the ages is, but how to question life so that they can arrive at their own values.

I wasn't particularly interested in teaching until I actually tried it. I was more focused on research, getting some kind of job in _____ or comparative _____ [subject areas] research. [Later in the interview:] But now I really like community colleges. I really like working in them and in the right kind of administrative atmosphere I would like to deal more with disadvantaged students. . . . I feel very good about teaching at City Community College. . . . To me the most important aspect of success is a feeling of genuine communication with students, that you can understand them as persons and they understand this and they understand you. And regardless of whether they failed to perform they've known that you were interested in them.

I always made an assumption—and this is where I very carefully planned—which is that I would teach high school for two years, go back and get my Ph.D. and become a very academic _____ [subject area] scholar [said with derision]. I no longer have any interest in doing that at all.

Interviewer: What was there that made you change your mind?

Teacher: Partly being an academic at the University of _____ [a prestigious university]. What I ended up doing there was a combined Master's in _____ and _____. And then I just realized that the primary concern there was how well you understood other people's ideas, secondary resources, and not really what your reactions were to the primary source. And I just thought it was, you know, absurdly bush league; I wasn't interested in doing that. And

I think also something like that is very straight-jacketed and the academics really tend to crush down, I don't know, creativity and spontaneity.... I think that if you were really academic that there's no place for you here, and that it would be very bad for you to be here.

Five of the seven faculty members who still conducted research did so not in their academic disciplines but in assessing and increasing the effectiveness of community college teaching. Rather than surrendering the research orientation, they redirected it in a fashion compatible with the career reinterpretations described earlier. For example, in one interview an instructor stated:

I now consider this publishing stuff a major part of my teaching career. The two are inseparable. You cannot do any publishing unless you are in a classroom, but I would not be happy just to be in a classroom, shall we say.... I've already talked with the publisher about some possibilities.

Interviewer: Aiming primarily at the community colleges?

Teacher: This is what I meant by classroom research as opposed to _____ [academic area] research. All of these are things where you've got to be in a classroom, and I [pause].... The material is right in the classroom with the students. I think it's the only way to do it, so that the students either understand what you're doing better in the particular course you're teaching.

Another teacher commented:

So two things happened [when he took a position at the community college while pursuing his Ph.D.]: one is I let my research slide and the other was I became enchanted with the personal contact of community college education, the contact with students.... There are two types of research, say for the sake of identification, research with a capital R, which is the Research which means that you were the first guy who got the thing done; and research with a small r, which meant that you discovered certain results but that somebody else had discovered them first. And our feeling was that to be a great _____ [area of study] you had to be a Researcher with a capital R; to be a great teacher, researcher with a small r was sufficient. In other words what you have to be able to bring to your students to teach them _____ was a feeling as to how you discovered things. It was irrelevant that somebody may have discovered them first.... Relatively little prestige is given to the art of teaching. My former colleagues at _____ University and I, we still talk about this, that the college professor is still probably the only profession where you're hired by one set of credentials and judged by a different set, that the concept of the kind of research that it takes to be a top-notch teacher still hasn't been solved. I mean, uh ... some place in between cut-and-dried methods courses and being a brilliant researcher in the field there are certain little things which may be God-given talents, they may be teachable, I don't know. But I mean that one of the things that I felt I was really doing was not giving up research but exchanging researches. I was going to stop researching in _____ [subject area] and start researching in people and teaching.

Of the two Ph.D.s who had rejected research, one said:

They [the administration] must have thought, "There's got to be something wrong with this guy." They just wouldn't believe that a man with my educational background would want to be in a community college. But teaching is my thing. None of that other stuff—research? Pffft! [He makes a sweeping motion with his hand, as if sweeping something from the table.]

The other nonresearch Ph.D. was more specific:

I'm not a writer. That is, I can do good research but I hate writing. I know I could produce, publish with pressure, but I just detest it and that is very appealing—to realize that you don't have that pressure on you.
    Interviewer: You don't have that at a lot of state colleges either, do you?
    Teacher: Probably not. . . . I would not be satisfied by just staying in a community college system and teaching basic courses. That I would find a bit of a rut. But why I'm very happy is . . . you know . . . uh . . . our department, we're creating curriculum for a program which will be a changing curriculum—part of the Human Services Program. We're going to have internships in community agencies. So in a sense I'm lucky I'm in the right department. You see what I have found is that my teaching has prepared me to do things that my degrees are not in, which I probably could not pull off at a large university. They'd say your degrees aren't in this. So from my point of view this is a very good place as a springboard to do a lot of things that I really don't have the credentials to do. And I know you don't really *need* the credentials, but you do, if you know what I mean.
    Interviewer: So you've undergone a rather interesting change in the sense that at one time you were thinking in terms of becoming an academic in a university. . . .
    Teacher: The other thing which I feel very happy about here is the lower- and lower-middle-class student; the lower- and lower-middle-class *white* student. He's really where the action is in time of—what's a nice word—consciousness raising.

In these retrospective interpretations of career transitions, the teachers described the erosion of old occupational commitments and the acquiring of new ones. In his discussion of occupational commitment, Becker notes that a commitment is indicated when, consciously or otherwise, a person has made a series of "side bets" (involving other facets of his life) on the anticipated outcome of his career.[8] The greater the bet, the greater the commitment. As we have seen, many of the liberal arts and human services teachers lost their bets—but not entirely. Still in the orbit of higher education, they could modify rather than abandon their commitments to a style of life, a set of values, and a definition of self. However disappointed or injured they may have been, they did not publicly identify themselves as "frustrated college professors." Indeed, a datum in itself was the frequency of teacher-initiated conversations in which the worth of the community college was defined and reenforced. The following are descriptions of such conversations as recorded in the field notes:

"My wife understood my reasons for leaving _____ [the university where he was a doctoral student]. But my parents and relatives thought I was crazy. They were also scared, thinking maybe I was asked to leave. But community colleges have some real pluses: The students are still establishment-oriented enough so that they are willing to try to learn through the system. There's no new left idea that you can't learn anything from lectures. The real affluent kids— like the ones at _____ University, they don't really think you could have anything to offer: 'He's only making $13,000. My father could buy and sell him.' But to the kids from _____ [the city] that's a lot of money. It says something to them."

He then briefly discusses the growing importance of community colleges. He says that originally they were founded to educate and train people who did not go on to or dropped out of four-year colleges. He adds: "Now the pyramid is inverting. More kids are going to community colleges and *we* are supplying the four-year schools or sending the students to work. They say in 20 years that four-year colleges aren't going to be that big or important anymore."

(overheard in the faculty lounge)

You know how I look at it? Working in a college is like playing major league baseball. Maybe someday you get an offer to coach a high school or even a college team. That's something important and maybe it's something you can't do in the big leagues. It's the same way with universities and community colleges. In a university you're playing, in a community college you're coaching.

(conversation while walking to class)

They [four teachers] strongly believe that an urban working-class community college is "where it's at." This last phrase was used by each of them.

*Smith: "Even if they are only in a vocational program, even if they say they are here only to get a better job, something else happens to them while they are here. *We can do something with them* [teacher's emphasis]."

In response, Jones says he remembers a cartoon in the newspaper that showed a southern man walking a large German shepherd. In the dog's mouth was the pant leg of a black man's trousers. The other half of the cartoon showed a northern woman walking her French poodle, the poodle nipping at the heels of a black man's shoes.

Jones: "The caption said, 'Up here we just nibble them to death.' One thing we may be doing here is not really raising their understanding, but just teaching them to nibble rather than bite." He explains that they may not really be changing the students, but just making them "less excitable."

Pierce says he sees the community college as a democratizing agency—providing avenues of mobility for working-class people. He complains that working-class people have been neglected in our system of education.

Adams complains about the president of the community college where he used to work, saying that the president is in the process of moving that school to a more middle-class community: "He identifies too much with four-year colleges."

(conversation in the faculty lounge)

After class, Durell said to me and Jones: "You know, a lot of times you see a kid as a freshman and you don't expect him to grow, but two years later you discover he's really changed. I know I felt that way the three years I taught at _____ Community College. Some of them can really surprise you. A lot of them come to a community college just filled with resentment."

Jones: "Like the kids who say, 'Why do I have to take a human relations course if I'm going to be a cop or a fireman or a pilot?' But if you can break through that resentment and get them to reflect on why it is important, sometimes that resentment can go away and the student can really *do* something while he's here."

(conversation in the faculty lounge)

Not only were such conversations definitional, but as socialization mechanisms they cultivated in the individual a sense of purpose, iden-

---

*All names used in this report are pseudonyms.

tity, and membership in the life of the group. In this process the teachers infused their work and their work setting with a sense of honor, dignity, and even superiority; at the very least they developed justifications for distinguishing themselves from the professoriate from which they were denied full collegiality.[9] Having become a community of fate (that is, having similar career dramas to resolve), the meaning of the new role and its position and function in the educational world were transmuted into a system of personal and communal bonds. As Peter Berger and Thomas Luckmann have stated:

> The transmission of the meaning of an institution is based on the social recognition of that institution as a "permanent" solution to a "permanent" problem of the given collectivity. Therefore, potential actors of institutionalized actions must be systematically acquainted with these meanings. This necessitates some form of "educational" process. The institutional meanings must be impressed powerfully and unforgettably upon the consciousness of the individual . . . institutional meanings tend to become simplified in the process of transmission, so that the given collection of institutional "formulae" can be readily learned and memorized . . . the objectivated meanings of institutional activity are conceived of as "knowledge" and transmitted as such.[10]

As evident in their remarks, for many teachers the "institutional formula" took on a sense of mission—to personally and humanistically open the eyes of their working-class students to new ideas. Although discussing the medical profession, Bucher and Strauss's statement concerning missions applies equally well to the liberal arts and human service teachers:

> It is characteristic of the growth of specialties [as it is with any professional or paraprofessional group] that they carve out for themselves and proclaim unique missions. They issue a statement of the contribution that the specialty, and it alone, can make in a total scheme of values and, frequently, with it an argument to show why it is peculiarly fitted for this task.[11]

That the teachers' battle for institutional recognition is related to the "identity work" described above is seen more clearly by examining the status of the community college in the structure of higher education. Since their inception, two-year institutions have operated in reference to two worlds—the public school system and the four-year institutions—without clearly belonging to either. In several respects this historical ambiguity has created a hybrid institution. For example, whether or not structurally associated with the state system of higher education, its traditional and philosophic ties to the local community are stronger than those of most four-year institutions.[12] Yet, despite advertising itself as an institution of, by, and for the local community, much as do comprehensive high schools, recognition that it is a qualitatively different institution leads the lay public, planning and accrediting agencies, and the "profession" itself to categorize the community college as part of the university and college system.[13] Another indicator of the community colleges' in-between status is that, although its courses are accepted for degree credit by most senior institutions, many of its students are not, and some students enroll only after having failed in a four-year institution.

Furthermore, although many community college symbols are borrowed from higher education, there is still some confusion. Language, for example, is used to invoke the image and aura of a senior institution. The titles within the academic ranking system are the same (instructor, assistant professor, and so on), but the degree requirements are not, as one can begin with a bachelor's degree and become a full professor with only a master's. In CCC, the teachers, with two exceptions, were not addressed as "professor" or "doctor" but "Mr.," "Mrs.," or "Miss" or by their first names; in addition, the chief administrator is not the principal, he is the president; his helpers are not the assistant principals, they are the dean of faculty, the dean of students, and the dean of the college.

These structural and symbolic ambiguities facilitate the career redefinitions of the faculty. Because in the community college teachers do not have to surrender the core component of their professional identity—that they are people who believe in and pursue intellectual activities—the teachers have only to modify the direction of this activity to fit the new context.

Most helpful in explaining how the teachers mesh expectations and reality is Gustav Ichheiser's, "Toward a Psychology of Success."[14] Ichheiser indicates that in everyday life the concept "success" has three meanings: reaching a desired goal, producing valued achievements, and getting ahead in the social space.[15] Because many teachers were not successful in terms of the first definition of success, they have modified and emphasized the second meaning and exploited the third. Specifically, the achievement most valued was no longer the production of knowledge but the distribution of knowledge, and furthermore, that distribution was seen as especially valuable because of its humanizing and emancipating impact on working-class students. (Indeed, in answering the question, "How do you define success in teaching in the community college?" teachers typically referred to past students who dramatically benefited in Horatio Alger fashion from a community college experience.) The third component of the success concept, moving ahead in the social space, is expressed in the way teachers capitalize on the school's ambiguous position by identifying themselves as in higher education and as playing roles equal to or more important than those played by professors in four-year schools.*

In short, although qualitatively different, the mission of the community college is made congruent with and supportive of the mission of senior institutions, thus allowing the teachers to maintain a measure of congruence between their once anticipated identities and their present function. (The similarity between this process and the "cooling-out" function is discussed in Appendix A.)

The theories of differential association and cognitive dissonance also help explain the changes in teachers' perspectives. In the first case, the teacher associates more with people who have a vested interest in redefining the career shift, and in the second case, the vested interest is the need to minimize postcareer shift dissonance in the organization of beliefs, attitudes, and values.[16] This process serves two complementary functions: protection against negative self-evaluations and increasing the attractiveness of the new career path.[17]

A major problem, however, was that these cooperative attempts to redefine, despite the structural factors that encouraged and facilitated them, did not work well. Ichheiser's comment is suggestive:

> If an individual thinks, or has the idea, that a certain event or a certain state of affairs is success, this by no means implies that, when immediately confronted by that event or state of affairs, he would experience it as, or even call it, a success.[18]

Recalling the observations of Becker and Strauss and Berger and Luckmann, we see that they too hinted at such a phenomenon. Becker and Strauss locate the source of strain in institutional arrangements: "The statement of mission tends to take a *rhetorical* form, probably because it arises in the context of a battle for recognition and status."[19] Berger and Luckmann, in their quoted passage, focus on the socialization process when they state that "institutional meanings must be impressed powerfully and unforgettably ... institutional 'formulae' [must] be readily learned and memorized."[20]

---

*As with halfway houses, rehabilitation centers of various kinds, and community colleges, interstitial institutions often serve to facilitate the processes of reidentification and status passage.

Learning and memorizing rhetoric or institutional meanings are not quite the same, however, as internalizing them, that is, making them a part of one's own system of beliefs and values such that they are fully congruent with one's self-conceptions. Indeed, as seen earlier, behind the teachers' declarations of allegiance to the community college credo lay nagging, private doubts that their careers had somehow soured. (The fate of these doubts is discussed in Chapter 5.) There were two reasons for this, the first having to do with the students' public unwillingness to work with ideas (discussed in the next chapter) and the second with additional factors in the structure of higher education. It is to the role of the structural factors that we now turn, beginning with a brief description of Martin Trow's analysis of mass higher education.[21]

Trow notes two major functions of colleges and universities, the autonomous and the popular.[22] Although all university functions ultimately are responses to societal interests, what Trow calls autonomous functions are those that the university, more or less independently, has defined for itself, those that are part of the traditional conception of the university. The three autonomous functions are the transmission of high culture, including the molding of mind and character, "the cultivation of aesthetic sensibilities, broad human sympathies, and the capacity for critical and independent judgement";[23] the creation of new knowledge through "pure" research and scholarship; and "the selection, formation and certification of elite groups: the learned professions, the higher civil service, the politicians ... the commercial and industrial leadership."[24] Inherent in these functions are values and standards that have become institutionalized in the universities and elite four-year colleges, and so survive even in opposition to popular sentiments, desires, and culture.

The two popular functions are the provision of vocational education to place people in the occupational structure and "the provision of useful knowledge and service to nearly every group and institution that want it."[25] The popular functions, in short, respond directly to the demands of the service-oriented occupational structure that began to emerge after World War II. According to Trow, it was this same period that witnessed the rapid growth of occupational education, so that:

> Throughout the class structure, already fully accomplished in the upper middle but increasingly so in the lower middle and working classes, "going to college" comes to be seen as not just appropriate for people of wealth or extraordinary talent or ambition, but as possible and desirable for youngsters of quite ordinary talent and ambition, and increasingly for people with little of either.[26]

Higher education in the United States, says Trow, has been able to fulfill both functions through a division of labor among and within institutions.[27] Many institutions are clearly oriented to the autonomous functions, selecting very carefully their students and faculty, sending their graduates to the more distinguished graduate and professional schools, and attracting revenue from institutions and individuals who wish to associate themselves with "high culture." By contrast, many colleges are primarily service or vocational institutions, "preparing youngsters from relatively modest backgrounds for technical, semi-professional and other white-collar jobs."[28] Included among such schools are the smaller teachers colleges, small, weak, denominational colleges, engineering schools, and two-year colleges.

Within those institutions that perform both functions, most notably the large state universities, various divisions of labor and people insulate and protect the autonomous from the popular activities. For example, there is a division of labor among departments, with some (for example, engineering) being more vocational than others (for example, history). In large public universities there is often a division of labor between the undergraduate and graduate schools, the former engaged in mass education, "in the service of social mobility and occupational placement, entertainment and custodial care," while the latter, "maintain a climate in which scholarship and scientific research can be done to the highest standards."[29] Trow also points to a marked separation between the collegiate, vocational, and intellectual student subcultures as contributing to the division of functions.[30]

A chief difficulty for many City Community College teachers was that the structure of their school, rather than insulating the autonomous from the popular functions, integrated them. The same teachers who taught a social science course to liberal arts majors might in the next hour teach a social science course designed specifically for human service or law enforcement majors. For example, the teacher who taught a sociology course for liberal arts majors, also taught a community problems course for human service majors (which covered such topics as housing, health, schools, community resources, and social agencies), and an urban society course for law enforcement students (which included vocationally applicable studies of crime, social disorder, racism, and ethnic and cultural differences). Another teacher taught liberal arts students an introductory chemistry course that was described in the catalog as follows: "Topics will include solution chemistry, acids and bases, oxidation and reduction, reaction rates and equilibrium, and introduction to methods in qualitative analysis." The same teacher also taught physics to fire science students: "An introduction to physical principles. The emphasis will be on practical applications as related to Fire Protection and Safety Technology. Topics will include mechanics, heat and electricity. *Note:* for students in Fire Science Technology Program only."

The content of such courses, then, centered not on an academic discipline but on the discipline's relevance to occupational training. In short, no more theory was taught than that necessary to understand the vocational uses of the field of study. (Several teachers attempted to teach more theory than the students thought applicable; the students' rebellion is described in the following chapter.) Occupational teaching is done in senior institutions also, but with an important difference. For example, when a class of nurses is taught the sociology of nursing it is usually under the auspices of the nursing or medical school and on its section of the campus. The instructor does not in the next hour teach the sociology of law to law students and then the sociology of community organization to social work students. Furthermore, when an academic department has one of its members teach vocational courses, this, too, is a division of labor; other members of the department remain insulated.

The integration of the autonomous and popular functions was symbolized by the arrangement of the instructors' work areas. Rather than having offices, the teachers had desks placed in the wide corridors specifically designed for this purpose. (The corridors were not ordinarily used by students but were plainly visible and easily accessible from the corridors they did use to move to and from classes. See the diagram of the floor plan in Appendix A.) Desk assignments deliberately mixed faculty across disciplines. The president of CCC did, of course, have an office, and while seated in it he explained: "The faculty are not seated by department because a feeling of community is more important than a feeling of department."

Walking along one of the faculty corridors one might successively pass the desks of an English instructor, a fire science teacher, a biology teacher, a law enforcement teacher, and a history teacher. While many regretted the diminished intradepartmental contact, the teachers cheerfully went along with the experiment. They did, however object to the constant surveillance by others:

> Putting the desks in the hall was a total disaster. The idea about the accessibility was good, but teachers need privacy too. The students had mentioned to me that they feel uncomfortable talking at those desks because they have no privacy. That has been a bad point from the students' point of view, and from the faculty point of view we have no privacy. When you're in class for a couple of hours, let's face it, you feel, just let me close the door and lock it for 10 minutes, eat

your lunch or something . . . have a cup of coffee. I don't know how anybody else teaches but I put on a show, not consciously, but unconsciously, and you can't let your mind wander for even five seconds. You have to be 100 percent for a full 50 minutes and that is terribly tiring, so I think we need the privacy too.

(a math teacher)

One thing that kind of grates on me is the desks where they are, out where they are. It's like being in a zoo. Aside from the noise and the distractions of the kids there's just no feeling of, well, you know, this is my office and if I want I can have the security of closing the door, doing what I want without being able to be seen by anybody who happens to walk by.

(a history teacher)

That continuous exposure and loss of control over social and physical contact can be an encroachment on the self has been noted by Erving Goffman[31] and, in reference to occupations, by Hughes:

It is probable that the people in [an] occupation will have their chronic fight for status, for personal dignity with [a] group of consumers of their services. Part of the social psychological problem of the occupation is the maintenance of a certain freedom and social distance from these people [the consumers] most crucially and intimately concerned with one's work.[32]

The absence of doors and walls also stripped away the possibility of being seen as a cloistered thinker. As one teacher stated:

It's just the idea that I don't have a door to close, that I can't do my work uninterrupted. Sure I want them to come talk with me when they need to, but it's not practical all the time. I might be able to do more good for more students if I could prepare a class without being interrupted. I think there's a matter of principle involved too. A teacher has to have a place to sit and think.

(an English teacher)

In summary, the teachers' dilemma was that having internalized the value of disinterested inquiry, whether in the classroom or through research or scholarship, they found themselves organizing, preparing, and teaching in reference to the popular functions. The collision of the two functions, for which most faculty were unprepared, in conjunction with the contrary student culture (Chapter 3) threatened self- and role definitions; in a subtle yet critical way these were assaults on the teachers' identities, and as such, had to be repelled. As described in the following two chapters, the manner in which this was done was, for some of their students, like salt in an open wound: It challenged the very sense of worth and ability they already doubted.

Nine of the 13 vocational instructors were interviewed. The critical factor in their move to the community college was a transitional period during which they began to remove themselves from their previous occupation's core activity (for example, police work, fire fighting, business), their new duties bringing them into contact with a community college administrator. A representative example is the career history of a fire science instructor:

> I graduated from high school in 1951 and I went into the service for four years as an enlisted man and I was in the fire department, fire protection and safety. Then when I got out in 1956 I went to _____ College and received an associate degree in fire protection and safety. From there I was in the fire department at _____ [city near City Community College] as a fire fighter. Then I went to work for an insurance company in _____ [another city near City Community College] inspecting fire departments. I worked for the rating association insurance people for probably eight years. I was appointed by Governor _____ to the State Fire Academy Commission as one expert in fire prevention control. . . . One of our duties was to see whether they should have a college program in fire science, and by being on this commission I met Dr. _____ [the president of a community college] because he appeared as a segment of higher education interested in fire protection. One thing led to another. He put me into contact with President _____ who was just going to start a fire program and he hired me to head up the program [here].

In three cases occupational contingencies moved the person to return to higher education (as an undergraduate or graduate student) where contact with a community college official was made. Reported a business teacher:

> After many years of excellent periods in the market [as a broker], making a lot of money, in '69 and '70 I recognized an unusually severe market break that, because of a lot of reasons, I felt would be a permanent change in the industry, that it was going to be much worse over the following years. Secondly, but predating even that was a real strong ethical conflict on my part. I just finally—you know, you go into any industry and you just get a partial view and I finally came to the conclusion that the brokerage industry was inimicable to the investors' interests. [He laughs.] And I got to the point where I wasn't willing any more to do aggressive selling, and to the extent that the brokers I knew who are still doing well I feel are whores.

Interviewer: With the change in the market situation was there a danger of your losing your job?

Teacher: Was there a danger of being unemployed? No. Was there a danger of having sharply shrinking earnings? Absolutely. I dropped more than 50 percent between '70 and '71. . . . So I then, after working for 10 years in the brokerage industry, I went to _____ College [a local business college] in the evening division while I was still working. I knew even when I started the master's program that City Community College was going to be built and I always had a kind of feeling that I was going to teach there. I answered a notice to teach one course in basic economics at _____ Community College and when the president of that school became the president here I made it a point to tell him that I was going to put in an application and that it was going to be the only place I would apply to.

In a similar fashion, a law enforcement teacher was facing mandatory retirement and a secretarial teacher's company was relocating; while taking evening courses, the necessary sponsors and contacts were met. As with the liberal arts teachers, the vocational instructors were not anticipating or preparing for a career in community college teaching; for the vocational teachers, however, the changes in status and image were not as difficult, although there were strains in breaking relations with old colleagues and establishing relations with new ones. For example, a law enforcement instructor told his class on the first day of school:

"I am Professor Smith, Professor John Smith, of the Law Enforcement Department. [He introduces the two other members of the department, referring to them as "professors"]. I worked in the _____ Police Department for 23 years, primarily as a detective. I spent 12 years in homicide, some of the murders I investigated are famous and I'm sure you've heard of them, and I also handled burglary and the shopping squad—checking fraud, forged checks, and other white-collar crime. I also taught at the Police Academy. ... Professor _____ [who he had previously told the class is a lawyer] will teach you constitutional law and I will tell you what is applicable in real police work. He will expose you to book work and I will teach the practical aspects." [Later in the field notes for the same class:] His grammar and diction are poor; one would never take him for an academic person—and I wonder if he considers himself an academic with his new position and his continuous use of "professor" to describe himself.

That he was actually "between identities" became apparent in this conversation overheard the next day:

A lot of my cases I left unfinished when I came here. Some guys came down yesterday from the downtown squad and they tell me to go with 'em to headquarters. They're tryin' to wrap up a case. I said to 'em [he breaks into a broad smile], "Listen, fellas, I'm teachin' in college. You gotta make an appointment with me now. [He laughs.] That really got 'em. I told 'em to call me 'professor' when they called. [More laughter.] But what the hell, they can't just come on down and expect me to drop everything.

With two exceptions (discussed below) the vocational instructors did not express career disappointment or resentment; rather, they were now preparing students to enter the occupational setting in which they once worked and the new distance from the vocation's core activity was subjectively viewed as upward mobility. Indeed, the increase in prestige was often directly associated with leaving behind the "dirty work" of the occupation. Said one business teacher:

I get paid for doing a job and I feel I'm doing a good job, and that's satisfying against a commission business where even if you're working hard you can wind up making no money and have the boss on your back during bad times. Also there's no more calling on clients to sell them what you know they don't need.

The law enforcement instructor who previously was a detective reported that his family strongly supported his career shift:

In their eyes it was a step up. . . . I really like teaching here. It's really great I can do this. But with my family, like I said before my father [also a policeman] was killed in the line of duty and I know my wife was glad to see the hazards gone. In the eyes of the police they said, "Why are you doing that?" They tell you on the police force, and believe me when I tell you this, that the thing to do is to come in, do as little as possible, and take home your paycheck. But I wanted the challenge, it's part of my constitution. The guys at headquarters when I come in say, "Oh, oh, here comes the professor!" [He laughs.] But I'm not walking the streets any more or getting any more blood on my shoes and this is the first time in 23 years that I don't carry a gun.

Similarly, a secretarial instructor stated that she is glad to be out of the office:

When I was a secretary for _____ [name of firm] I liked it. I met some really interesting people. But on the other hand I'm not "the girl" any more. If there was a problem [in changing occupations] it was that in the office you're told what, how, and when to do something. When I began teaching they said it was my course and I could teach it any way I wanted, it's up to you. That was a pleasant change, even if it means taking work home.

The two exceptions mentioned above were two lawyers, one a law enforcement teacher and the other a business instructor. Neither had worked in the occupational setting for which they were preparing their students. To the contrary, both passed the bar examinations the year CCC opened and, after much searching, were unable to find work as lawyers. For example, one applied unsuccessfully to the military service, to regulatory agencies, and to utility companies. Unwilling to work for a large law firm or to open his own practice, he had a relative in the community college system who, acting as his sponsor, helped secure an appointment in the business department:

> I took as many different kinds of courses as I could in law school. I didn't concentrate in any one area. The basic courses in law school in preparation for the bar exam involve a lot of business topics. Most of the subjects you take have a lot to do with business, corporations, tax real estate. Just the whole contracts course—most of the contracts are business contracts. So I had that kind of background and when I was interviewed here I told them I was interested in both business and the law enforcement department. And I guess they didn't want to straddle me, they didn't want to have me teaching out of both departments. . . . At first I felt a little like I wasn't using my legal education and I still feel that way to a certain extent. Being involved in the business department, taking part in all of the things that go on in it, and you know a lot of it isn't really that related to law.

The chairman of the business department also had an atypical career path that is worth describing at length because of its relation to the program he would institute. After receiving a bachelor's degree in business administration, he worked two years for a large accounting firm and then attended a theological school and spent the next 25 years as a Protestant minister. During that time he earned a Ph.D. in religious education and delved seriously into the philosophy of education and the psychology of learning. His interest in teaching began as an avocation leading one or two courses per year in the junior and senior colleges in his town.

> I taught accounting at _____ College for two years. That was almost accidental that that happened. I thought I was going to be teaching a course in philosophy, but the vice president decided to keep it himself and said rather accidentally, "We need somebody to fill in in

the field of accounting for a guy on sabbatical," and because I had the undergraduate background I took it. . . . I had maintained this expertise insofar as it was usable to me in the management of the churches I've served. . . . Since I was teaching in the business department I started doing some studying and began to realize a revolution was going on in the business field, for instance, of contract teaching, or this psychological contract between, say, manager and his employees, that would enhance the worth of the situation. So, in other words, my behavioral science and educational backgroud in sociological psychology, the whole matter of human relations and how people function and the philosophical implications that would come from philosophy and theology. So after five years in _____ where I was teaching part time, I finally gave up trying to get into the philosophy or psychology departments because I was real excited about where I was, and actually my life came into focus there. I had the basic business background of finance and accounting and I had the behavioral aspect and those two things really matched in modern-day business. As a matter of fact I think it's quite remarkable what courses— I think there's a matter of divine guidance in this thing that I didn't fully understand—but nevertheless, my education is specialty and generalist in the world today and I have the theological, philosophical, behavioral, finance-accounting; quite exciting to me, the combination. I said to myself, here I've been a parish pastor for 25 years and, incidentally, very excited about it, not turned off by it, but I said to myself, two things; one—where is our society being molded in this day and age? It used to be home, church, and school as the primary place, and I concluded that the primary genesis of values in our society today are government and business and the media, and that if I wanted to be where I could help shape society—and that's the only reason I went into the ministry in the first place; I was a liberal Protestant who was out to reform the world, to remake the world, and if I wanted to use my life where it could impact the world most significantly, I really had to be, not in the cloister, not hidden in the school, as important as those may be, and the family's almost overwhelmed over what's going on in the field of values today, but I had to move into business and government and the media, and I realize I already had a major foot in the business world and that if I could focus my ministry—and I make no apologies for the fact that I'm . . . it isn't known by my students—I don't have any reason to keep it from them, but I also know they would stereotype me if they knew what I was and I'm not interested in being put in a box by anybody. I'm only interested in functioning as a human being with whatever expertise I come with as a human being. I don't keep it a secret, but I don't wear it on my sleeve and I'm not looking for it to be published . . . but obviously if they see my resume it's on there. So I decided that I would move into the public areas of life.

At this point in his career he returned for 30 hours of postdoctoral work in the application of behavioral sciences to business management:

> I think I could have academic credentials as a scholar, but I am primarily an activist, a practioner, a doer. . . . At _____ University I was in a training sequence that used to be called sensitivity training, and I wanted those particular skills to use them as teaching skills both in the classroom and in a school such as this and as a consultant. . . . I have begun a consulting practice and finally, now in 1974, I have a very exciting teaching job that gives me the opportunity to bring all of my expertise into teaching.

Unable to find a job in a university, his graduate school mentor told him "the exciting, cutting edge of education is in the city college":

> I didn't believe him then. I believe him now. I saw the junior college as a kind of compromise. . . . You were smarter, better if you were at a four-year college, and furthermore, if you were really smart you'd be at the graduate level. It was probably prestige, a status situation, but now I realize the tremendous role that exists here.

Although not expressing (or unwilling to express) career disappointment, his history clearly distinguishes him from the larger group of career teachers. Indeed, his desires meshed well with the vague "humanizing" mission of some liberal arts teachers. As we shall see, his reaction to student opposition to academic work was similar to that of certain liberal arts instructors. The difference was that he instituted a formal program to deal with the opposition, a program which was imbued with some of the basic premises of the perspectives of most liberal arts teachers.

The differences in the career paths of the vocational teachers were expressed in the classroom. Just as they were, in a fundamental sense, non- (or less) intellectual, so were their courses. Rather than asking their students to manipulate abstractions, they instead asked for the learning of discrete bits of information; there was little or no need to generalize beyond specific facts. These courses were cut, dried, and packaged. Lectures were often taken from the text and reported verbatim, and students were frequently given in advance the questions and answers to the multiple-choice and true-false examinations.* In such classes students were not expected to intellectualize. The liberal arts courses, on the other hand, were geared more to conceptualizing and to analyzing problems by degree.

---

*The secretarial students developed their typing skills through a series of tape recordings that guided them through progressively more difficult exercises.

In summary, the descriptive data in Chapters 1 and 2 relate the various dilemmas of students and teachers to education, career, and social class. The accompanying tensions, if not completely resolved, had to be managed in some fashion; in this sense they were important determinants of perspectives. We turn first to students' management of these concerns (Chapters 3 and 4) and then to the teachers' attempted solutions (Chapter 5).

NOTES

1. For statements concerning the link between careers and identities, see Howard S. Becker and Anselm Strauss, "Careers, Personality and Adult Socialization," *American Journal of Sociology* 62 (November 1956): 253–63. See also Everett C. Hughes, "The Sociological Study of Work: An Editorial Forward," *American Journal of Sociology* 57 (March 1952): 423–26.

2. Everett C. Hughes, "The Study of Occupations," in *The Sociological Eye: Selected Papers* (Chicago: Aldine/Atherton, 1971), p. 295.

3. Becker and Strauss, "Careers, Personality and Adult Socialization," p. 263.

4. Although the career path is not yet institutionalized, an increasing number of universities have programs to train new and in-service community college instructors; in 1954 there were 23 such programs and in 1968 there were 75. Still, the vast majority of present two-year college instructors have not completed such a program. See Arthur M. Cohen and Florence B. Brawer, *Confronting Identity: The Community College Instructor* (Englewood Cliffs, N.J.: Prentice-Hall, 1972), pp. 148–54.

5. Howard S. Becker, "Notes on the Concept of Commitment," *American Journal of Sociology* 66 (July 1960): 38.

6. As Hughes has stated: "Our aim is to penetrate more deeply into the personal and social drama of work, to understand the social and social-psychological arrangements and devices by which men make their work tolerable, or even make it glorious to themselves and others." Everett C. Hughes, "Work and Self," in *The Sociological Eye: Selected Papers* (Chicago: Aldine/Atherton, 1971), p. 342.

7. Again, Hughes has stated: "Subjectively, a career is the moving perspective in which the person sees his life as a whole and interprets the meaning of his various attributes, actions and the things which happen to him. This perspective is not absolutely fixed either as to points of view, direction, or destination." Everett C. Hughes, "Institutional Office and the Person," *American Journal of Sociology* 43 (November 1937): 404.

8. Concerning the phenomenon of committing oneself to an occupational identity during the early stages of the career, Hughes has pointed out: "A person's conception of himself is itself something of a stereotype, to which parents, teachers, siblings, peers, and his own dreams have contributed. Some people project themselves far into the future, others operate more or less in the present. But in either case, there come moments of necessary revision and adjustment of one's notions about what he can do and wants to do. One may say, then, that a young man thinking about himself as a physician is thinking about a young man as yet unknown to himself, doing work and playing roles not yet known, in situations he has never yet been in. This is not to underestimate the anticipatory playing of roles; but no matter how sensitive the individual's anticipation of himself in a future role, there is some gap between anticipation and realization." *Men and Their Work* (Glencoe, Ill.: Free Press, 1958), p. 126.

9. Rue Bucher and Anselm Strauss have observed, "Whom a man considers to be his colleagues is ultimately linked with his own place within his profession." Rue Bucher

and Anselm Strauss, "Professions in Process," *American Journal of Sociology* 66 (January 1961): 330.

10. Peter L. Berger and Thomas Luckmann, *The Social Construction of Reality: A Treatise in the Sociology of Knowledge* (Garden City, N.Y.: Doubleday, 1967), pp. 69–70.

11. Bucher and Strauss, "Professions in Process." p. 326.

12. Christopher Jencks and David Riesman, *The Academic Revolution* (Garden City, N.Y.: Doubleday, 1968), pp. 481–83. Jeanne Binstock has pointed out that the community college yields to every variety of local pressure: "The domain of the public junior college is the most narrow of any type of college. Its constituency and its concerns are local. Since all residents of a district have a right to attend, a public junior college operates under one particularly severe constraint: the administration cannot control input and any decision as to the institution's goals and effective socialization procedures must be based on a given constituency which is absolutely unselected as to motives, traits and abilities and which is outside the control of administration." "Design from Disunity: The Tasks and Methods of American Colleges" (Ph.D. diss., Brandeis University, 1970), pp. 191–92.

13. Leland L. Medsker, "Changes in Junior Colleges and Technical Institutes," in *Emerging Patterns in Higher Education,* ed. Logan Wilson (Washington, D.C.: American Council on Education, 1965), pp. 79–84.

14. Gustav Ichheiser, "Toward a Psychology of Success," in *Appearances and Realities: Misunderstandings in Human Relations* (San Francisco: Jossey-Bass, 1970), pp. 168–200.

15. Ibid., pp. 171–74.

16. E. N. Sutherland, *Principles of Criminology,* revised by D. R. Cressey (Chicago: Lippincott, 1955), pp. 77–80. Leon Festinger, *A Theory of Cognitive Dissonance* (Evanston, Ill.: Peterson, 1957).

17. According to the variant of dissonance theory advanced by Deutsch, Krauss, and Rosenau, to avoid postdecision dissonance not only must values, beliefs, and attitudes be balanced against each other but a person must protect himself against implications that are contrary to his self-definitions. Morton Deutsch, R. M. Krauss, and Norah Rosenau, "Dissonance or Defensiveness," *Journal of Personality* 60 (1962): 16–28.

18. Ichheiser, "Toward a Psychology of Success," p. 170.

19. Bucher and Strauss, "Professions in Process," p. 326. Emphasis added.

20. Berger and Luckmann, *The Social Construction of Reality,* p. 70.

21. Martin Trow, "The Transition from Mass to Universal Higher Education," *Daedalus* (Winter 1970): 1–42.

22. Ibid., pp. 2–4.

23. Ibid., p. 2.

24. Ibid., pp. 2–3.

25. Ibid., p. 4.

26. Ibid., p. 3.

27. Ibid., p. 4.

28. Ibid., p. 5.

29. Ibid.

30. Ibid., p. 6.

31. Erving Goffman, *Asylums* (Garden City, N.Y.: Doubleday, 1961), pp. 24–25.

32. Hughes, "Work and Self," p. 345.

3
TENSION MANAGEMENT
AND PERSPECTIVES IN
THE COMMUNITY COLLEGE: THE
TRAINING PROGRAM STUDENTS

The concerns brought by students and teachers to City Community College were not the sole determinants of perspectives. Equally important were the contingencies of the school situation itself. More specifically, the definitions on which conduct was premised were a product of the interplay between day-to-day interpretations of community college life as well as concerns of identity and social class.[1] For students, this can best be understood by examining how they took into account, in their daily round of activities, the roles, values, and demands of their teachers. As detailed in the previous chapter, the "autonomously" oriented liberal arts and human services teachers were concerned that students intellectualize, that students manipulate abstract concepts independently of concrete occupational applications. While these teachers were not unappreciative of their vocational students' aspirations, they did expect their students, regardless of major, to acquire a broader, more analytic and flexible view of the human condition and/or a more scientific view of the physical world. The vocational or service-oriented teachers, on the other hand, were concerned with training.

The essential problem for training program students was that the different expectations and pedagogies of these two groups of teachers exacerbated self-doubts concerning mind, intelligence, limited social mobility, and what these said about oneself.[2] The essential problem for students in the "autonomous" programs was that intellectualizing implied upward mobility and, as shall be seen, this status change was also translated into a statement about oneself and was both feared and welcomed. The central point is that for students in both groups academic activity was a problematic feature of community college life as it was bound with issues of one's fate, of one's niche in the social world, and hence of what membership in a status group implied about oneself and one's social honor. (The concept of social honor as operationalized by students and its relation to social class is discussed later in this chapter.) As the analysis of field data will reveal, the worth of ideas and the idea of worth were inseparable issues.

The problematic nature of training and intellectualizing meant that the role of student could not automatically be enacted, but rather had to be devised by students in accordance with interpretations of these problems.[3] In other words, the way the student role was played was both a response to immediate situational demands and an attempt to manage dilemmas of identity and class. These problems required students to judge how hard to work, on what to work, and for and against whom to work. The resulting role-governing norms provided students with guidelines for regulating effort, budgeting time, and, as shall be seen, for resisting teachers. In this manner students operationalized the perspectives that dominated the life of the institution.[4] This chapter considers the training students; Chapter 4 deals with the liberal arts and human service students.*

As previously described, the information presented in training program classes (law enforcement, fire science, executive secretarial, and business administration) corresponded very closely with textbook assignments, with lectures frequently read from the textbook and exam questions and answers given in advance. The following field notes describe a typical law enforcement class:

> The classroom fills from back to front. Smith calls the roll in a military fashion. Twenty-seven present, 15 absent. He begins lecturing, actually reading, from notes. Most students have their books open to follow the lecture. Few take notes—they know better now. . . . Smith's grammar is still very bad—this is regrettable stereotyping, but he talks like a cop: "There is much valuable information in this here handbook. One of these informations concerns. . . ." The lecture is on stopping and searching suspects. As he talks he tells the class specific points that will be on the test next week. . . . Smith reaches the end of his lecture notes and I can see from looking at Bill's textbook that it corresponds with the end of the chapter. Many students close their books and prepare to leave although the hour is not yet over.
>
> Smith: "Where are you going?"
>
> There is sudden silence and he continues discussing the test. There will be 20 questions on the test, he says. He then gives them the page and the paragraphs from which the questions will be taken.

---

*The human services vocational courses were to be offered in the second year. Since the fieldwork covered only the school's first year, the reactions of the human services students to their vocational courses are unknown. They are considered in this report along with the liberal arts students.

At one point he stops to say that he will continue giving the questions for the next few minutes; as he continues I see many students smiling at each other.... As we leave the classroom, Tom says to me, "He couldn't make it any easier."

(a law enforcement class)

Skills were also taught. For example, secretarial students spent many class hours learning shorthand, typing, and correspondence formats:

Kern reviews the procedures they should use in the shorthand homework assignments. She also tells the class which warm-up typing exercise to do before class so they will be "rarin' to go" precisely as class begins. She then says, "Some of you have not handed in your lab work. [Lab work consists of students' taking dictation from a tape recorder.] I know who you are. I have a record...." She begins teaching new shorthand symbols. The students repeat after her. She gives dictation. The class does several typing exercises. Then the process is repeated. The drills require the students to type a business letter dictated in shorthand using the proper format. For one of the drills she asks the class to recite together one of the letters. The class recites slowly and in a low voice. Kern: "The trouble with you folks is that you come in here after lunch and it makes you sleepy."

(a secretarial class)

The repetitive and mechanical nature of this work made it possible for teachers to make frequent use of tape-recorded lessons and drills:

Each student (all of whom are female) sits at a typing table and takes out a shorthand notebook. The tape begins and in accordance with the instructions the students write various shorthand symbols. The voice on the tape is male; he begins each exercise, "Write as I dictate." Several exercises are repeated. The teacher does little as the recording progresses except to walk quietly around the room and peek over the students' shoulders. The exercises are very repetitious.

(a secretarial class)

Similarly, business students were required to master various elementary marketing procedures as well as accounting methods and skills:

They take out their workbooks and using sample cases are shown how to make different kinds of entries into ledgers. All the students are working along with the teacher. He asks several questions about the entries and students answer readily. The class is very mechanical, consisting of where in the ledger to put different kinds of entries, such as debits, credits, and accounts payable. This goes on for 90 minutes.

(a business class)

In these courses, then, the students were not asked to synthesize abstractions or to exercise critical faculties. In the humanistic sense this was not "education" with the emancipation that that implies, but rather was a series of mental and physical tasks. According to Stanley Aronowitz:

> The community college student becomes aware that he is receiving an inferior training, much less education, by the content of the courses. . . . The student does learn that he has been deceived once more. The endless waiting in the lower grades for a different education that was supposed to be fulfilled by college is followed by the recognition that college is not meant to be a fount of wisdom, but is, at best, a credential for a job.[5]

As seen in Chapter 1, Aronowitz is not quite right, for students, correctly or incorrectly, felt more deceived by and disappointed in themselves than in the quality of their secondary schools. Indeed, it was because they had "waited" in the lower grades that they were now uncertain of themselves and distraught in their current situation. Enrolled in training programs, they did *not* expect school to be a "fount of wisdom" and, importantly, this awareness led them to compare what was wanting in their programs with what they believed to be wanting in themselves.

The comparisons these students made revealed an ambivalence toward self and situation that was most clearly expressed in their responses to the manner in which they were taught and tested. They both liked and resented the straightforward presentation of facts, whether by machine or by human teacher. It was liked, as the following field notes illustrate, because the repetition of discrete bits of information or the demonstration of simple skills was a predictable and orderly system within which to work:

> Smith [the law enforcement teacher] is alright that way. He tells you what's on it [the test] so you can write it down. He tells you it's from page 97, paragraph 2. You've got to be stupid to fail that course.
>
> (a law enforcement student)

Pierce reviews Chapter 9, telling the students what to expect on the tests. For example: "The following will show up on your exam—take it down just this way." Whenever he does this the students look at each other and smile broadly as if congratulating themselves in advance for doing well on the test. One student blows on his fingernails and polishes them on his chest.

(a law enforcement student)

The best thing about it [a business course] is that you know what's going to be on the test. It's self-paced so you take it when you want to. You never have to panic the night before.

(a business student)

Some of his multiple choice questions can be tricky as hell, but I know just how to prepare for it. I mean I always know what's going to be on a test from what he says in class, so you never have to worry too much about psyching him out.

(a fire science student)

There's nothing to learning business letters. If you type one six times you know it so you can pass a test. I have to practice typing. Same with filing and shorthand. It's all easy. You just do what she says in class. It's easy that way.

(a secretarial student)

This same orderly, mechanical approach was resented by students because, they thought, it pointed to their limited abilities. This is evident in the following remarks in which students draw connections between subject matter, pedagogy, and self-definitions:

Shirley said you'd have to be a moron to flunk a secretarial course. Dianne replies, "Are you proud of that?" and explains that since you'd have to be a moron to flunk it doesn't take "much brains" to pass.

(two secretarial students)

Bill: Shit, that was boring. It's the same shit in the book.
Dave: That's what you gotta do just to be a lousy cop.
Bill: I bet you didn't have to learn all this shit to become a cop 20 years ago.
Dave: Cops weren't lousy then.
Bill: Ya.

(conversation on the way out of
a law enforcement class)

Costello [the lawyer who teaches the law enforcement students] asks if Smith [the ex-detective who also teaches them] gave back their last exam. When a student answers yes, Costello asks if Smith reviewed the test in class.

Student: "It was too simple to go over in class." There is no laughter or other response from the class. As they are dismissed I hear Bob say to Joe: "They give simple tests to simple people. I knew I should have gotten into liberal arts."

(a law enforcement class)

Joyce said that next semester she is switching her major from business to liberal arts: "Business is so boring and dry. And it's so easy. I never study and I'm getting an A. It's not challenging at all. You have to be pretty down on yourself to stay in that program. I can do better than that."

(a business student)

The class is given a break from their accounting exercises and I go with Ray and Roy to the hallway.

Ray: What a waste!

Roy: Let's split.

Ray: No, let's stay. It's only another half hour.

Roy: No. I'm going home. I don't want to stick around here. You have to be an asshole to stay. I'm sick of their exercises. You comin'?

Ray: No.

Roy: Then you're our resident asshole.

(two business students)

These courses, then, presented a moral conflict: To do well required engaging in mechanical behavior incompatible with self, but to do poorly reaffirmed the existential bete noir described in Chapter 1. The common solution was to redefine the institutional definition of doing well in a manner that protected students' sense of social honor. This code of honor was expressed through behavior that symbolically put forward a claim to both peers and teachers that one was a person possessed of dignity and self-esteem in that one's unwilling compliance was not cheaply given.

Like the threats to self-determination, will, and efficacy, which, as Erving Goffman has demonstrated, give rise to the resistance and underlife in total institutions, the students' informal code of honor redefined the official expectations: "of what they should be putting into and getting out of the organization and, behind this, of what sort of self and world they are to accept for themselves."[6] Specifically, where attendance was expected, absenteeism prevailed; where enthusiasm, low levels of effort; where honesty, cheating.[7] Each form of resistance will be discussed in turn, but first it is necessary to examine an additional factor, the vocational students' experiences in their nonvocational courses.

As noted in Chapter 1, students in the different training programs were required to take specified courses in English, the social sciences, and mathematics, as well as a varying number (depending upon the major) of liberal arts electives.(Fire science students, in addition, were required to take chemistry and physics courses.) From the first day of school the teachers of these courses made it clear in class that, as described in Chapter 2, they value intellectualizing and would expect it from students:

> He compares the intellectual's love of an idea with a male's courting of a female. He tries to give the students some idea of what an intellectual feels as he "falls in love with an idea," how this is followed by a "pregnancy," and then an "intellectual birth." He concludes, "This is what social science is all about."
>
> (A social science class for
law enforcement students)

Most teachers were not this obvious, but still made known their value orientation. For example, from the very beginning of each semester two teachers frequently referred to books they had authored, one teacher continually referred to his graduate school as "*The* University," two teachers frequently dropped the names of their prestigious graduate schools, and almost all teachers began the semester by presenting and analyzing abstractions. One English teacher began her course by giving the titles and authors of the several assigned books and then asking, "How many of you are familiar with existentialism?" The only response was three students laughing.

Thus by stressing the value of intellectual activity, the liberal arts teachers became, in effect, another reminder of what the vocational students thought to be their own shortcomings. Again, the students saw social mobility as a matter of personal responsibility and hence believed that people with the drive and the talent achieve social distinction. The training students, then, became wary of their liberal arts courses and teachers as indicated by these three law enforcement students discussing their urban society teacher:

> Mike: Edwards is too smart to be teaching here. He should be at a real college. He should be at Harvard or Yale. He even looks that way with his sports coat and patches.
> HBL: What do you mean?
> Mike: He's really intelligent and sometimes I can really get interested in what he's saying, but it doesn't relate to anything. Like I don't know why he's talking about it in the first place. And some-

times he'll be talking and then switch to something completely different and I don't get the connection.

George: I think he ought to be some place else. He's even got his
Ph.D.

Larry: No, he has his doctorate. He said in a couple of classes
that he was against the war and in radical politics like SDS and that
bullshit. I don't hold that against him because he's probably over that.
But that and what Mike says about him being intelligent, it just goes
to show you the difference between him and us.

A similar theme was struck when I asked a group of business
students why they rolled their eyes and wore a look of disgust every
time their government teacher mentioned one of her books:

Sheila: At first I just thought it was interesting because I never
knew anyone who wrote a book. But the more she talks about it the
more I think she's putting us down. I mean I get angry. It's like
saying, "I wrote this book and you couldn't write a book so you listen
to me."

Paul: It's a holier than thou attitude. Any teacher can make you
feel that. No matter what you do, they always have that over you.

HBL: Have what over you?

Paul: Their education. Most of my teachers are nice enough
people, especially Huber, but they have this way of making you feel
like shit at the drop of a hat.

Given these concerns, resistance to the "intellectual" teachers required
additional measures. Where assignments were to be read and written,
they frequently were not; where class discussions were anticipated,
there often was silence; where classroom decorum and deference were
expected, there was incivility. These measures and their functions will
now be discussed.

CHRONIC ABSENCE

Absence was seen by some students as a means of dissociating
themselves from slavish adherence to official expectations and as such
was often positively redefined:

Len and Don decide to go home even though they have two classes
this afternoon. Len wants to work on his car and convinces Don to
help him, but only after some resistance. At one point Len said it
wasn't "cool" to go to class as much as Don did. I ask what he means

and he tells me that if you go to every class you're seen as a "brown-nose," trying to curry the teacher's favor.

(two law enforcement students)

Jerry: "Mr. Crane asked us how come we're absent so much so I gave him some crap about working and Tom told him he has mono."

HBL: "Why, wasn't that true?" Jerry says that he only works two nights a week and that Tom does not have mono: "Sometimes I think I don't go because they want me to go. If I went to every class I'd feel like a dope."

I ask why he would feel like a dope.

Jerry: "Nobody goes to every class. You don't have to. You can borrow somebody's notes and besides, I'd be too studious if I did." The word "studious" is said with derision.

(A business administration student)

That students stayed away from classes does not necessarily mean that they stayed away from school. As in most schools, socializing in the lounges, cafeteria, and hallways was a popular pastime. As a class hour approached and a group decided not to attend, their justifications often referred to the defiance of indignities:

After lunch they decide not to go to Pierce's class but to play Ping-Pong in the "pit" [the game room].

Bill: "He's so fucking boring. He just stands there with one leg up on the desk and lectures. Why the hell don't he do something interesting? I feel like I'm a writing machine taking down notes on shit."

(A law enforcement student)

The four of them decide not to go to their English class.

Pete: "Just before our big English exam, remember when Dumont [the teacher] said, 'And don't insult me with any of your poor spelling.' "

George: "She said that? Man if I was there I would have said, 'Fuck you.' " He stands up and raises his middle finger.

Laura: "I felt like saying, 'And don't you insult us either.' "

Mea: "They do insult us. Look, we all know we're not the best students in the world, but who wants to hear a teacher explain the difference between there, their, and they're. [Laughter] I can't stand that. Who wants to listen to a dissertation on punctuation? That's why I don't go to class anymore."

(four business students)

I sit with Steve and Ian in the lounge. We talk about hockey for a while and the bell rings. They decide to skip Ashley's [a social science teacher] class. After a few more minutes I asked what they thought of Ashley.

Ian: "The first week of classes she told us about her background, how she taught at some exclusive private school. It seems the whole semester she's been talking down to us like she was on some kind of platform. I know a lot of guys don't like that. You can bet your ass that's why we're not in class right now."

Steve agrees.

(two fire science students)

Alan tells Frank you have to be "a sucker" to go to Robertson's [a business teacher] class more than once a week: "It's just facts, facts, facts. Learn this, learn this, learn this. All you gotta do is find out from somebody what you have to know to pass the module test." He says again that only "a sucker" goes regularly, and that "I'm no sucker."

(A business student)

LOW LEVEL OF EFFORT

Not doing reading and writing assignments or volunteering for class discussion was more common in the vocational students' liberal arts courses. From their perspective, minimizing effort was not seen as laziness or indifference, but rather as the proper stance to take to avoid self- and peer derogation. It was not a question of being unmotivated, but of being motivated by interests at odds with the teachers' expectations:

A student asks Ryan [a social science teacher] about the book report assignment. Ryan says it is not due for three weeks but he wants them to read it now.

Student: "But I don't want to read it now if I have to report on it later. I'll forget it."

Ryan: "Actually I want you to read all three books now."

The class laughs.... As I walk out with Tom and George I ask why they laughed at Ryan's request.

Tom: "I couldn't be a bookworm if I tried." He says he tried to read the first book but it was "weird" and "I didn't understand it." He adds, "So why should I knock myself out?"

I say that if he tries to read it slowly the book might become clearer. He reminds me of yesterday morning's conversation about it taking him a few days to learn how to use a lathe properly [for a summer job] and that every time he made a mistake he was embarrassed. "If you had that job and never learned how to use it, wouldn't you be embarrassed?"

I say I would and he replies, "Well, I've been going to school for 13 years and I didn't understand the first chapter of this book." He holds up the book Ryan assigned, "So why should I read chapter two?"

(a business student)

Penn [an English teacher] discusses the book: "This is not a 'how to' book: it's more of a 'wake-up' book to get you to look critically at how you use your own language, both written and oral language." She explains they are also to examine how printed and electronic media use language. She adds: "It is necessary to react as college students to Hayakawa [the author of the book]. Increasingly you will learn you are expected to react critically, not accept what you read as gospel, to use your own intellectual abilities." She discusses the importance of language in terms of extending self-awareness and awareness of others. She asks a question about why word choice is important. There is no response. She asks again. Silence. Finally she calls on people. . . .

[After class] I have lunch with some of the students in the class. As we're going through the lunch line, Bill picks up a sandwich, puts it down and picks up another one, saying very derisively, "I reacted too critically to the first sandwich." Laughter from the others. Later at the table I wonder out loud why nobody wanted to answer her questions. Fred says he knows one question he'd like to ask her. Laughter. Bill says, "Because it's not important. . . ."

[Later when Bill and I are alone] I ask him again about Penn's class and I say that I've noticed students' reluctance to respond in other classes. Bill says that one reason is that it just isn't "cool" to speak up too much in class, especially to volunteer: "Everybody would give me a case of the ass if I did that. It's OK once in a while except when a teacher comes on strong you've got to back off a little."

I ask what he means by "comes on too strong" and he answers that it's when they ask you to do too much work. I say, "But she was only asking you to answer questions."

Bill says it's the kind of questions she asks, "They're too academic. I'd feel funny answering them." He then says he is angry at her anyhow because she only gave him a C+ on a paper: "I copied the goddamned thing right from the encyclopedia. You know, I changed a few words around. She writes some shit on it tearing it to pieces. The only one who gets an A is this 65-year-old bag, Rosy. She gets an A and I get a C." This last remark is said with much disgust, as if a 65-year-old woman shouldn't be able to do as well.

(a law enforcement student)

Rock shows me a reprint of an article by Bloom [an English teacher] that was given to everyone in Bloom's class. Their assignment is to read the article and grade it.

Rock: He's been giving me C minuses and that's just what I'm going to give him. Why should he get any better than I do. I'll get my thesaurus (he pronounces it "thesaurisis") and cross out words left and right and use some others like he does." Rock is angry and obviously insulted. "Just look at the title and that will tell you what kind of guy he is." He gives me the reprint, points to the title and says, "Translate that for me!" The title is "Linguistic Camouflage—Euphemisms Are In."

Rock: "Now who the hell wants to do anything for a turkey like that?"

(a law enforcement student)

Leo: It's not like I feel superior or snotty myself, but the students here just don't seem to work very hard. I remember when I was in high school we took books home and did some studying. Don't get me wrong. I don't want to give you the impression I study hard. It's like this. The teachers here have a way of emphasizing that tells you what's going to be on a test. The pressure here is minimal. You go to classes, don't you think it's easy? I think you'd find that the opinion of most students here is that it is very easy. You take Smith's class. We have reading assignments, but no one does them. Why should we? He's never asked us a question in class yet. Costello's class is one of my toughest, but even there I don't do much reading. Actually, I don't know what effort is anymore. The only way I can tell what effort is, is to see what everybody else is doing, and most everybody is doing nothing. Most people don't do anything until exam time, so is the little I do effort? And if things keep going this way I think I'll get 4 Bs and a C. I think that's pretty good, don't you? So if people don't work here it's because students don't pressure each other. . . . I don't feel like I have to compete: the best thing is just to get by and to make out OK without putting yourself to the test.

HBL: What test?

Leo: I don't mean a *test* test. I mean getting by without studying. Let's face it, if there was a lot of pressure here most guys wouldn't do good and would have been out of school at the end of the first semester.

HBL: Do you mean there's sort of an unwritten agreement that students won't work hard?

Leo: Well, I suppose, but it's not really that. It's more like most guys couldn't do anything hard anyhow. Look, none of us are what you'd call your basic bright student.

HBL: In other words, if nobody really works hard then everybody's safe.

Leo: That's right.

(a law enforcement student)

Among the training students there was no division of labor whereby students would delegate responsibility for different assignments. Friends did willingly share notes with, of course, the expectation that the favor would be returned. They also would help prepare each other for vocational tests by asking objective questions from a written list. Although this required some involvement with course material, students were careful to avoid giving the impression of being inordinately involved in their work by commenting on the mechanical nature of their preparation in a fashion that dissociated themselves from it:

> I come across John helping Mo prepare for this afternoon's test. John is asking Mo a series of questions that Smith has said would be on the exam. Several times Mo answers the questions before John is through asking them. When Mo does this, John says, "Holy shit" or "Jesus." At one point John comments that Mo must have read the book carefully. Mo answers he hasn't read it all, that he only was concerned with memorizing the answers. He adds: "So there's nothing amazing about it. It doesn't take any smarts."
>
> (two law enforcement students)

> Jerry tells Roberta and me that he is going to take his business module exam next period. I wish him good luck and he says he won't need any because he memorized the answers yesterday with another student and has gone over them earlier this morning. He shows me the list of questions and I ask him two which he readily answers. He comments, "See, nothing to it."
>
> Roberta: "Pretty proud of yourself, huh?"
>
> Jerry: "For what? Memorizing this? Anybody could do it."
>
> (two business students)

> Jean tells me she prepared for her typing test by typing each kind of business letter three times. She says "What a drag, you just do it and it sinks in." I ask if she likes it that way since it seems so easy. She replies that it is terribly boring but she forces herself to do it.
>
> Sue: "There's no other way to do it. You just duh, ya know sit dere and, duh, play with da machine." As she says this, she apes the mannerisms of a dunce.
>
> (two secretarial students)

CHEATING

Cheating was common but not universal. In some classes few students cheated and in others most of the class was observed cheating; some students never cheated, others only occasionally, and some at every opportunity. (Cheating is defined here as obtaining information from other students or from crib sheets; an added complexity is that

although many noncheating students were observed to notice others
cheating, I learned of only two such cases being reported to a teacher.)
For many students cheating was another way of dissociating themselves from their work. Implicit in their comments is the idea that
while getting by is important, one's work should not be taken too
seriously:

> Tom asks me: "You're not coming to our class today, are you?"
> HBL: "No, why?"
> Tom: "We're having a test; you absolutely would not believe
> the cheating." Laughter from the others.
> "That's for sure," says another student.
> Tom: "Man, you *gotta* cheat to pass this. You can't learn all that
> shit she wants you to unless you read the textbook all day. And I'll
> be damned if I'm going to do that."
> Vinnie: "There are better ways than that to spend a day unless
> you're like Ted and don't mind being a good little boy and do your
> homework. I seen him yesterday in the library with his workbook.
> Shit, I had workbooks in the third grade."
>
> (a group of business students)

> Regan gives the quiz. There is much cheating, with students craning
> their necks to see each other's answers. A female student gets halfway
> out of her desk to examine another student's test. A number of stu-
> dents are whispering and I see six students peeking at their lecture
> notes. Two are using crib sheets. I am still seated next to Harry and
> notice that he has trouble answering some of the questions. After
> several minutes, he looks at Pat's quiz and answers the questions. As
> Joan walks out, Harry whispers to her, "Number one?" Without hesi-
> tating Joan gives him the two-word answer to question one. Regan,
> meanwhile, has not looked up from whatever he is writing. . . .
> After class Harry tells me that cheating is common. I think his
> unsolicited comment was his way of once again making sure that I
> can be trusted. I say that I know it's common and "I wonder why it
> is."
> Harry: "Because if you did everything they wanted you to do
> you'd have to spend too much time studying. You've seen the stuff we
> have to do. Does it look interesting to you?"
> I ask if people cheat only because they don't like the subject. He
> says there are other reasons (such as having to work, just being lazy,
> putting off your work, trying but not understanding), but that cheat-
> ing also has to do with how boring a subject is. "If you get interested
> in something, then you don't have to cheat. You do the reading be-
> cause you like it."
> I ask why people can't work at something they don't like and
> Harry tells me that some people do, but for him it just isn't worth it
> to bore himself.
>
> (a business student)

INCIVILITY

The last means of resistance was incivility.* According to the *Dictionary of Contemporary American Usage,* a civil person is one who behaves dutifully,

> especially in the observance of those forms and ceremonies which serve to preserve the peace ... he abstains from rough and abusive language, gives to every man his due, and observes all common forms of general respect for others.[8]

Approximately one month after school opened, students began violating the peace by injecting *sotto voce* taunts into class lectures and discussions. Importantly, these indignities were directed at two kinds of teachers—those who taught liberal arts courses and those who taught vocational courses but were clearly identifiable as middle-class persons. For example, law enforcement students did not harass their two teachers who were ex-detectives, but they did make life difficult for the lawyer who taught the legal aspects of police work, as seen in these excerpts from four different classes:

> Costello [the teacher] begins by saying he wants to discuss a short newspaper article on the death penalty. He reads the article and says, "It would be interesting to discuss the death penalty, wouldn't it?" Three students say "No" rather loudly, look at each other and smile. Costello begins discussing the death penalty as if he hadn't heard their remarks.

> A student asks if they should take notes.
> Costello: "No. It's not necessary for this material. Just relax."
> They do relax. They make a big show of closing their books and stretching out. Costello asks if he has already explained *McCulloch* v. *Maryland* to this class. Some say he has, others that he hasn't. Meanwhile they are all looking at each other smiling: many are fighting laughter.
> [Later] Lou tells me he did explain the case before, but that they were just razzing him.

> Costello says that under the circumstances just described a suspect cannot be searched. Then he says he has made a mistake, a suspect

---

*Using incivility as a datum does not require this author to judge "proper" classroom decorum, for as shown below, the students themselves clearly knew they were being disrespectful. Indeed, only with a knowledge of proper classroom behavior could they use improper behavior for their purposes.

can be searched. In unison the class says, "Oh-Oh." Their tone is derisive. One student says, "Let's stab him . . . oh!" and clutches his chest. Costello just continues, although red-faced. Many of the students are smiling almost joyously at each other, as if they have just pulled a fast one.

Toward the end of the class Costello begins to discuss when a policeman can legally draw a gun. Brian interrupts rather loudly: "There are three times when you can draw a gun."
    Joe (very satirically): "Tell us!"
    As Brian recites the three reasons Joe says "Uh-huh" after each one. It seems that Joe is out to irk both Costello and Brian [who had a reputation as the teacher's pet].

Similarly, fire science students did not taunt their ex-fireman teacher, but they did guy their "eastern" educated chemistry teacher, as in these representative scenes:

As the class ends, she says, "Your assignment is to read pages 129 through 139 in the text." Ron says loudly, "Ya, we'll do that." A few students snicker.

She asks if they had any difficulty with the homework problems. Someone in the back of the room says very derisively, "Oh, no, they were very easy." Laughter.

It is not, of course, that law and chemistry are unrelated to police work and fire science, but that these courses emphasize "theory" rather than practice. In this fashion *sotto voce* remarks frequently punctured the English, social science, history, and math classes. In these classes taunts were usually an immediate response to a teacher who either was stressing the value of working with ideas, acting too "intellectual," or, worst of all, disparaging working-class people. In each case they were reminders to the students of what they thought to be their own limited capacities and social worth. As the following vignettes illustrate, the students thus became engaged in a symbolic crusade whereby they could defend their honor by assaulting that of their teachers:

They are reviewing for tomorrow's final exam. At one point Delaney [a math teacher] says: "With the exception of some multiplication problems, we didn't go beyond addition in this course. Oh, well." She reviews some laws of addition and multiplication: the distributive, the commutative, the additive inverse, and the additive identity. She asks if anyone read last Sunday's *New York Times Magazine*. No one has. She says there was an article last Sunday on the new math, "which is just what we've been doing in this course." She then returns to a problem they were working on. I can see what is coming. The students have just been told that, "Oh well, we've only done addition," and then asked if they read the *Times.* It doesn't take long. In response to one of Delaney's questions, a student satirically says, "Come on, you tell me the answer. I want to learn." There is laughter from several others.

(a math class)

Lionetti begins by saying "We'll go over the [business math] formulas today so that *somebody* knows what's going on." [His emphasis] He begins explaining the formulas using data taken from an article on the cost of oil during the fuel crisis. He almost loses control over the class as the students inject rather silly jokes about the crisis. Finally he says, "OK, we won't go over the formulas and you'll all get a zero on the test without my help." The class suddenly becomes quiet. On a purely subjective level I see expressions of anger in some students' eyes, but there is no other reaction. After a few minutes Lionetti says that knowing about interest rates is important to them because "buying on time is part of the American way of life and you should know how much you're paying when you charge something." He then makes his *faux pas.* He asks if they have credit cards, "like Master Charge." Laughter.

Male student: "Oh, we all do." He reaches for his back pocket and simulates taking out credit cards: "Bank Americard, American Express." More laughter from the students.

Another male student says, "They won't give them to us."

Lionetti continues the lesson calculating the cost of credit. Some male students in the back of the room are fooling around, poking each other and talking. After three minutes during which Lionetti talks over them, they quiet down. At one point he gives them a formula, $I = PRT$, and tells them he will demonstate how to use it, "But I won't get into the theory behind it because, well, let's try one out."

Frank says caustically, "Yeah, let's try one out."

Another male student satirically to Frank: "What are you, a wise guy?"

Lionetti takes them through the formula. . . . He says, "Look, this question is so simple I shouldn't even ask it—if one pays three quarters of a percent per month, how do you figure how much one pays per year?" The students are having great difficulty with this and they are continually disrupting the class with jokes and side conversations. Lionetti is exasperated a couple of times, as students not only disrupt but fail to answer correctly the most simple questions. Lionetti asks a question, a student answers, other students interrupt with their own answers until finally Lionetti says, "Let me put this on the board."

A female student says, "Yeah, help us out." Giggles from the males.

Lionetti whips around, "I'd rather you helped yourself, I'm not going to do all the work for you." He does not shout but he does raise his voice. Throughout the class he is struggling to maintain control. . . .

Joe answers a question. He has trouble finishing the answer. Another student, "Let's see you get out of this one, Joe." Laughter from the other males.

At another point, after Lionetti explains something to the class, a male from the back of the room says loudly, "Somebody's got to remember this for Tuesday [the day of the test]." Much laughter from the class.

(a business math class)

Palmer [an English teacher] distributes copies of a short article from the *New York Review of Books* by Alfred Kazin on the political and ideological uses made of the American flag by the working class. For the first few minutes she analyzes the structure of the essay and the writing techniques used by the author. The students (most of whom are law enforcement majors) are asked to pick out key sentences. The conversation soon turns to the substance of the article and six or seven students (about one-third of the class) begin one of the liveliest debates I've heard all year. Palmer takes a liberal stand, vehemently criticizing government secrecy, Watergate, the Asian war, the 1968 Chicago convention, and inflation. She makes her disgust evident. Four people support her statements. It wasn't until she made a key mistake that students began opposing her. The mistake was siding with Kazin in opposing the "unthinking, fanatical working-class hard hats." She reads the following quote to buttress her statement: "This particular segment of the working class most features crane operators and other lordly specialists who from the heights of their well packed pay envelopes look down on blacks who can't even become plumbers' apprentices."

She then says: "We've been talking about the working class, but maybe we ought to get it straight what we mean by that. What would be an example of a high status occupation?"

A male student gives a closed fist salute and says defiantly: "In my neighborhood construction workers have high status." A number of students cheer. Palmer is red-faced and agrees that status varies with neighborhood.

Another student says: "We have some rich people moving back into _____ [the community where City Community College is located] and fixing up the big old houses. They're all weirdos—flaky."

Palmer asks: "Why do you feel like that?"

Student: "The same reason you do. Class prejudice!" Four or five male students cheer.

The discussion quickly returns to the anti-U.S. statements made earlier. The students defend the United States, saying how we've supported relief efforts and spent billions on foreign aid to ungrateful nations. A number of small debates erupt simultaneously. The class is out of hand. Palmer herself is engaged in a side debate. She tries to quiet the class, but they act as if she is not there. One student tells her to "sit on it."

(an English class)

Foley asks the class to distinguish among reports, inferences, and judgments (terms used in their textbooks). There is no response. She calls on students and they obviously do not know the answers. One student finally offers a partially correct answer. She berates the class saying, "You haven't lived up to your responsibility as good students and as long as you don't you can expect me to be bitchy." At the word "bitchy" the class gasps satirically. She ignores this and goes on with the lesson by asking the class for descriptive adjectives. One student says, "I'd like to give you one, but I can't say that," implying that his adjective is obscene.

A few male students snicker and poke each other in the ribs. She has difficulty quieting them down. Some of the students prepare to leave too early—they close their books, stretch, put pencils in their pockets. The talking continues. Foley yells, "Let me have your attention please!" I see some of the students looking at each other with impish smiles on their faces. During the last three minutes she has to speak over the students.

(an English class)

I see Lasky in the hall and ask to sit in on his class. After he consents, I ask, "This is basic math I, isn't it?" He says softly, "Base, basic math." He laughs and shakes his head.

He begins by announcing a quiz for next week and adds, "I hope the homework exercises will do more good than harm. If you don't have good study habits to begin with they could hurt you. I'm sure some of you will get even more confused." He begins the lecture by saying they will work today on adding, subtracting, and multiplying negative numbers. He says he does not want to begin by showing them how to compute negative numbers but rather will begin on the philosophy behind their use. He offers a long discourse on Descartes and the era of enlightenment. After he begins the discussion of computation he at one point asks for the sum of 7 plus 3. There is no response from the class. He asks again, astounded at the silence. After a moment a student says "10." As he turns to write on the board I see a few students smile at each other. Two students hold up 10 fingers and nod their heads, feigning seriousness. Another student makes a show of counting on his fingers to 10.

(a mathemathics class)

At the beginning of class a student asks Lionetti how they did on the test, to which he replies, "I think a lot of you know more than you show." He explains they are going to begin something that will be important to them—"something you will be able to use a lot." He begins explaining percentages, how they are notated, for example, the difference between .2 and .02, how to move the decimal point, and so on. Later the class has great difficulty changing fractions to percentages.

Lionetti asks: "Phyllis, how do you change 3/8 to a percent?"

Phyllis: "I don't know."

Lionetti: "No idea?"

Phyllis shakes her head no. Lionetti gives the class a formula: "This formula will come back to *haunt* you." He gives the class exercises to do. After a few minutes he says, "Ellen, what are you doing?"

Ellen says sheepishly: "Nothing. I don't know how to do it."

Lionetti reexplains; his tone is friendly and patient. Then he says: "You have to learn to think about it. I can't keep on telling you how to do it step by step. You've already forgotten what we learned in the last two weeks about decimals and fractions. Is that the way you do it? Learn it and forget it?"

Steve laughs and says somewhat hostilely, "Ya!" Two others laugh—apparently at their own inability. They scratch their heads as they realize they don't know how to do the problems.

In reexplaining how to change fractions to decimals, the fraction 1/20 is put on the board. Lionetti asks: "Does this ring a bell?"

Student: "Five percent?"

Lionetti: "Right. What is one twentieth of a dollar?"

Student: "A nickel."

Lionetti says in an undertone: "I hate to ask real obvious questions, but sometimes I get scared." For a moment the class silently stares at him. A student flatulates very loudly and the class roars with laughter.... On the way out of class, Tom (the offender) is congratulated by Nick and George.

Nick: "You sure got him good."

George: "Atta baby Tom, you really socked it to him."

Tom: "Oh, man, it couldn't have come at a better time."

(a business math class)

Scenes such as these were commonplace, occurring daily in liberal arts courses taken by training program students as well as in those vocational courses taught by the lawyer and the chemist. (Exceptions are discussed below.) These incidents indicate that for students there existed two competing definitions of the situation. The first was that they were in school to do something for themselves and this required cooperation with and acquiescence to the teachers' definitions and requests; when oriented to this definition classes proceeded smoothly and without interruption. The second was the more negative definition described earlier in which students were induced by the machinations of the social class system to assume responsibility for their current predicament; when oriented to this definition, often as a reaction to a teacher's words or manner, students counterattacked. To the extent that students were always subject to being discredited, classes were always precarious, always potentially subject to the disruption of a competing definition of the situation that momentarily devalued the worth of what they and their teachers were doing and saying. The students, in this fundamental way, were expressing what was ultimately a social class dilemma.[9] By angrily pricking the authority of the teacher's definition of the situation, students were confirming that they all knew "something was going on underneath," and, perhaps most importantly, taking action on this collective realization was seen as honorable. Indeed, the wry smiles, knowing looks, and self-congratulations expressed both pride and joy in the momentary abandoning of acquiescence, in the momentary exercise of power, will, and autonomy. Thus, in this social class struggle in miniature, taunts were the weapons by which minor victories of dignity could be won.

Absenteeism, limited effort, and cheating served a similar function, for as seen in the remarks of students, these measures, when taken together, gave substance and a sense of solidarity to the different groups of training students. The function of such behavior was to demonstrate that each student was part of a collectivity worth belonging to because it protected the most intimate interests of its members. In taking a stand together they in effect instituted a code of honor much like that described by Georg Simmel:

> Such a code would imply that every member of the group would feel that his honor was diminished whenever any member suffered an insult or a deprivation of his honor. . . . Hence, criteria of honor in all their intricacies became the symbols of social groups. Status honor even exists in the negative sense. This status-dishonor, so to speak, allows for a certain latitude of behavior, which is regarded as human enough or even as honorable. . . . This negative code permits deviation from, just as the positive code of honor adds demands to what is already generally expected. . . . As a result the same demand can receive two emphases which are quite different. It may be the maxim of an individual not to suffer insults in silence, but he will act on this maxim in private life one way, and in quite a different manner [in public life]. . . . This elaboration of special codes of honor for different status groups reveals one of the most important, formal sociological developments. It manifests itself a thousandfold in a wholly rudi-

mentary manner, in mere nuances of feeling and acting and often disguised by motives of a more personal or materialistic kind.[10]

To be unconcerned about "dignity" in the face of self-doubt was to leave oneself vulnerable to uncomplimentary and even degrading peer and self-evaluations. There were of course some circumstances in which students did not feel their "honor" on the line and consequently did not retaliate. In one case a math instructor often reminded students of his working-class background, identification, and sympathies:

> Several times during the hour he says such things as "When I grew up in _____ [an inner-city community adjacent to City Community College]," "There's nothing like living with people who know what life is really about," "In my neighborhood you had to learn to be tough to make it," and so on. He also uses profanity freely and manages to make several allusions to local sports heroes in a manner that indicates that he is to be taken as quite the opposite of a "stuffy" academician.

In general, for a teacher to avoid students' gibes he had to have been what the students were becoming (for example, a policeman, detective, fireman) or convince them that "he was one of them."

An interesting variation occurred in the business program. In the skills courses (for example, accounting) in which students learned specific, concrete, demonstrable routines, they did not taunt their teachers, but rather sat attentively, asked pertinent questions, did assigned drills, and, in general, were cooperative. When the *same* teachers taught the theory courses (basic economics, marketing), however, their position was analogous to that of the lawyer who taught the law enforcement students and the chemist who taught the fire science students. As the subject became more abstract, the definition of the situation changed and there appeared such scenes as the following:

> Shaw returns the marketing tests and says the grades were low. The students make rather loud sounds of disgust as they receive their tests. There is much aggressive talk and play—two students are hitting each other in the arm. They blurt out questions concerning the test. That is, they do not raise their hands but literally shout out questions: "How was it graded?" "Will there be a makeup test?" "What was the class average?" These questions are asked one after another with Shaw having no chance to answer one before the next is asked. If there is such a thing as conventional classroom manners they are little in evidence.
>
> (a marketing class)

Crawford asks how the energy crisis will affect marketing. He is bombarded with shouted answers, some serious, some silly. There is much laughter and a number of wisecracks. For example, Crawford asks a question and I overhear Pete say the answer (in a low voice) to Ray. When Crawford answers his own question using the same idea expressed by Pete, Pete responds by shouting, "Hey, you can't say that, I just said it." Crawford is taken aback. Pete and Ray laugh. Crawford asks other questions and in the midst of the continuing pandemonium, a student will occasionally try to answer seriously. As Crawford lectures, the students shout out such things as "Save fuel by taking showers together," "Assassinate the president so he won't be flying all over the place." Crawford can barely control the class. After 20 minutes of this, the students quiet down and Crawford lectures.

After seven to eight minutes many side conversations develop. One student continues to make comments very loudly while Crawford discusses the oil crisis. Examples: "Don't worry about the oil crisis—drive a bike ... go to Florida ... buy a horse ... get some Alaskan huskies ... it's warm in Florida ... I've always wanted to go horseback riding, Tally Ho!" Occasional laughter. Crawford ignores all this banter.

At one point Crawford is talking about the price of crude oil per barrel; he asks, "Forty-five is the price, isn't it?"

Student: "Ya, that sounds about right." He then puts his hand over his mouth, laughs, and whispers to a friend, "What the hell is he talking about?"

As students ask and answer questions, side conversations and wisecracks continue. The students seem to be enjoying this. Crawford goes on as if nothing is wrong. Finally, he says, "Look, you don't have to attend class. If you want to continue talking, go somewhere else!"

Student: "Ya, you guys, we're having a class discussion." (Student laughs.)

Another student: "Ya, this is very important" (hides laughter). He then shouts, "There is no gas shortage, it's a gimmick. If they can't find a place to store it, they can put it in my backyard. There's no shortage, it's just the government ripping us off."

Another student: "Hey you guys, you don't have to attend class!" Laughter. This last comment is obviously a reference to Crawford's earlier plea.

Another student shouts: "Get a guinea president up there; we'll all get stiff on wine and we won't have to worry about the heat." These comments are made while Crawford continues talking.

Crawford asks students to open their books. "Are there any questions on the reading?" Students sit and talk, seemingly oblivious to Crawford. With an exasperated look on his face, Crawford asks again; no response. He asks: "Do you know what chapter it was?"

Students: "Fourteen."
Crawford: "Right. Are you ready for the quiz?"
Student: "What quiz? It's not until Friday. Let's discuss the oil
crisis." (Laughter).
        Crawford asks how many read today's case—8 of 22 have. They
discuss the case. No note taking.

                                                    (a marketing class)

Gibes were limited to the more intellectual and abstract courses
because students appreciated that in these classes there were no routines to be learned, no questions and answers to be memorized, and that
it was more difficult to cheat on essay examinations. They had to fall
back on their own diligence and intelligence, yet they doubted both.
Once again, the nature of the material to be learned was a reminder of
a doubted self, and anxiety was thereby exacerbated and collectively
expressed.

NEGATIVE CASES

In reference to absenteeism and limited effort there were three
groups of students who established different norms. First were the fire
science students, half of whom were already full-time firemen. They
had an immediate incentive to do well in that graduation meant an
increase in both pay and the possibility of promotion:

"I just told my wife last night that I've never studied so hard or did
so well when I was in high school. It's because I have a sense of
direction." He says that if his courses at City Community College help
him get a promotion he'll be even happier. And if not, he says at least
he'll be getting more money for the same work.

                                                    (a fire science student)

The half who were not yet firemen were displeased by having to work
so hard, but felt they had to keep pace:

There's something in it for those guys [who are already firemen], but
I work my ass off with no guarantee. Even if I pass the civil service
exam I could be unemployed, especially if the blacks get first crack.
So I try to keep up with everybody, but they have an advantage
because they already know things I don't.

                                                    (a fire science student)

Despite their serious approach to fire science courses, in the nonvocational courses (for example, social sciences, chemistry, English) they

were like other vocational students in their absenteeism and restricted effort:

Terry and Jim are complaining about their English teacher. Terry turns to Mel: "We had a quiz where we had to define the different terms. It wasn't an open book test, but I opened the book and put the definitions into my own words. I still got half of them wrong. She wants too much. I don't do half of it."

Jim says, "She probably still thinks she's at _____ [a nearby university]."

Terry: "Is that where she was? I always knew she was a bean-bag."

Jim: "She's not like Dave [the math instructor who identified with the working class]. He was able to adjust after he got out of _____ [another university]. It just shows that it's a lot harder to teach here. You're not teaching the brainy ones here."

(two fire science students)

The second negative case were the secretarial students who had to attend class regularly to acquire typing and shorthand skills. They, too, had an additional incentive in that they could begin looking for a job once these skills were obtained. As explained by one of their instructors:

"We haven't had much of an absenteeism problem in the secretarial courses because it's the kind of course you can't cut too much. It's not like if you didn't do the reading today, you can do it tomorrow. We're working with a skill that has to be developed over time and through practice. Most of the girls realize this." She tells me it's problematic for a student to decide at what point she has enough skill to get a job. The longer they stay the better job they can get, yet some lower-level jobs are always available. "They have to analyze their own needs and the market needs very carefully. Some girls have already left us to take jobs."

Yet, despite this incentive, the secretarial classes, unlike other purely vocational classes, were often ruptured, as in these two examples:

Crosby [the teacher] begins to explain today's lesson but many students are still talking. She asks three separate times for them to quiet down. Even after the third time there are four simultaneous conversations among the students. Finally, she says, "Girls, please!" They stop for two or three minutes, then four students resume whispering. Crosby answers a student's question.

After the explanation, another student says loudly and in a mocking tone, "How many times does she have to explain it to you." They laugh. The tape begins—the girls learn and write various shorthand symbols.... A student whispers loudly, "Oh, I want to go home."

[Later] Crosby says, "I want you to begin lesson four now and finish it tonight." A student asks in a very complaining tone of voice, "If we do lesson four tonight what will we do tomorrow?"

Crosby: "We will have plenty to do tomorrow."

Student: "Oh, I thought you would say we didn't have to come to class." No laughter. Three students smile at one another.

Another student: "Can we go now?"

Crosby: "No! You can begin the lesson here."

(a secretarial class)

Ajamian [the teacher] asks them to shut off their typewriters and prepare for a short quiz: "It's not on something you've never heard of before. We've gone over these things numerous, numerous times. I just want to see if you know them." She asks questions. The students talk among themselves.

Teacher: "Absolutely no talking."

A student asks, "Can we whisper?" Laughter and more talking. Someone makes a joke I cannot hear—more laughter. Three more times the students make jokes above the quiz questions Ajamian is asking.... The students groan at some of the questions—half in seriousness, half in jest; the groans are overexaggerated.

Ajamian: "Make sure you're doing your own work, please." The questions are all mechanical, concerning formats, spacing, fingering, and so on. For the third time she says, "No talking, no talking whatever."

She mentions a brand name of stationery and a student yells out from the third row, "What kind was that?" As she answers and continues her explanation of the business letter format, some students are talking.

Ajamian: "Do you want to talk or are you going to listen to me?"

The two students continue talking. She yells, "You probably want to talk, but I'll make you listen to me." The students are quiet for a minute but again begin talking once the quiz ends and they are instructed to continue their typing. I cannot hear what they have to say over the din of the typewriters.

(a secretarial class)

Thus, unlike the students in business, fire science, and law enforcement (89 percent of whom were male), the secretarial students (95 percent of whom were female) exhibited overt "resistance" in their vocational rather than in the liberal arts courses. Indeed, in their liberal arts courses secretarial students were cooperative, attentive, polite, and, in the collective judgment of their teachers, among the brightest and most willing to do academic work of all the students in the school. This inversion can be explained by examining the social class and life situation differences between the two groups. For purposes of comparison, let us contrast the secretarial and the fire science students.

Fifty-eight of the 80 female secretarial students (72 percent) either were from one of the seven wealthier communities of the 14 communities discussed in Chapter 1 or from an affluent suburb.* Only 6 (17 percent) of the 35 male fire science students were from such communities. In reference to life situation, the mean age of the secretarial students was 19 and of the fire science students, 27.5; while only four secretarial students (5 percent) had husbands, 21 (60 percent) of the fire science students had wives. Furthermore, most of the secretarial students lived with their parents, while the firemen were more likely to own homes or live in their own apartments.† For the fire science students, then the present and the future were less problematic. The secretarial group, having a higher social status and a less certain fate, were more concerned with detaching themselves (through classroom behavior) from the uncomplimentary implications of their work—specifically that the low status value of a secretary's "mechanical" work implies downward or no mobility.

That the threat of downward mobility was a very real concern for the secretarial students was seen in their attitude toward the male students in the school:

> I ask them [three secretarial students] if the guys in the school are the kind of guys they would like to marry. They emphatically say no.
> Debbie: "They have no class, no sophistication I mean, who cares about driving around in a souped-up drag machine."
> Pam: "I have a word for them—gorillas. The school is full of them."
> I ask if this includes the guys in the liberal arts courses.
> Debbie: "Not so much. They're bad, but not like the law enforcement group. They're totally unsophisticated."
> The three of them consider it highly unlikely that they would marry someone who had not gone to college. I ask if they think the guys might be turned off by females who appear to be smarter.

---

*Again, it must be cautioned that these are ecological data and that the socioeconomic characteristics of each student are not known in detail.

†Although the business and law enforcement students were only slightly older (a mean age of 20 for each group) than the secretarial students, they, too, came from the lower-income, less educated communities. The data on students' age and residence were furnished by the school administration.

Mary: "Well, you know, you're supposed to act dumb to keep a guy and I admit to doing that, but not with any of the guys here because they're not my type. Most of them are very immature."

Pam: *"Very* immature." Pam tells me she was in a two-year dental hygenist program at _____ University but had to drop out because of an accident. She now hopes to get a job in a law firm or "a business with a good reputation." I ask what her father does; he is an electrical engineer, white collar. I ask if she would consider marrying a policeman or a fireman. She says that you never know what will happen, but she seriously doubts it.

I ask about the students in the business program, and Pam replies, "You've got to understand that most of them come from ____ ___, _____, or _____ [three nearby working-class communities]. Most of them don't know what they're doing in business and they won't go anywhere most likely. I just can't see them really becoming anything."

I ask, "So you kind of rule them out?"

Mary: "I guess we have prejudices against them."

In part, the strength of these "prejudices" was reflected in the seating patterns in those liberal arts classes the secretarial and male vocational students took together. In 29 of the 34 such classes observed, the students sexually segregated themselves as they took their seats. Figure 3.1 depicts some examples.

The third negative case was a small group of older students (approximately 40 in number) in the Business Administration, Executive Secretarial, and Law Enforcement programs. On all measures—absenteeism, restricted effort, cheating, and incivility—they were very much unlike younger students. Because older students formed their own cliques with qualitatively different perspectives, they are discussed separately in the following chapter.

In this chapter the relationship between social psychology and social class has been investigated. Implicit in this analysis has been a joining of Meadian and Marxist social theories, both of which postulate the existence of a dialectic between the individual and society. In their study of blue-collar and lower-white-collar workers, Richard Sennett and Jonathan Cobb have stated in this regard that the social psychological impact of class

is that a man can play out *both* sides of the power situation in his own life, become alternately judge and judged, alternately individual and member of the mass. This represents the "internalizing" of class conflict, the process by which struggle between men leads to struggle within each man.[11]

FIGURE 3.1: Samples of Seating Arrangements in Vocational Students' Liberal Arts Courses

```
        T                               T
- - - - - - m m m -       - m                                    m
- - - f f - - - - f       - - m                               m
    f f - - f f f -       - - - m                          m
      m m - - m m -       - - - - m                     m
                                      f f f f f f f
                          - - - m m f - f f f f - - - -


        T                       T
- - f f f f - f           - f f - - - m
f m f f f f f - m         - f f f f - m
- m f f f m m - f         m m m m m f
- m m m m m - - f


        T                       T
- - - - f f f f f - - m   - - - - f f f f
m m - f - - f m - - - f   - f f - - f f f
m m - f - - m - f m m m   m - - f m m - - -
- m f f f f - - - - - m   - m m m m m m m f
```

f = female, m = male, T = teacher, – = empty seat.

By ignoring the consequences of class, one risks the oversight made by K. Patricia Cross in her study of urban working-class community college students (whom she collectively refers to as "New Students"). After combining data from several national surveys in her first chapter to show that "New Students" are indeed working class, she all but ignores the possible impact of this variable and concentrates instead on students' psychological characteristics and academic abilities. She concludes:

> New Students as a result of their constant battle with failure in the school situation, are more fearful of putting their abilities to a test than are their more successful peers. They have learned that learning involves risks to the ego. There is, after all, always the chance that in approaching any new situation—which is the essence of learning —they might fail. Whereas the past experience of good students tells them that they probably will succeed, the past experience of poor students tells them that they will probably fail. According to theory, one set of expectations results in achievement-oriented personalities whereas the other results in failure-threatened personalities. Success-

ful students are motivated to try; unsuccessful students are motivated to protect themselves against the threat of failure by not trying. They seem to say, "If I don't try very hard, I can't fail very much."

The attitudes of New Students support the theory. They are less confident of their abilities; they avoid risk situations where possible; and they are more likely than traditional students to obtain passive scores on a scale measuring the tendency toward active or passive approaches to life and its demands. For New Students, the school situation has been a fearful experience, and the lessons they have learned are handicaps to future learning.[12]

In one respect the training students of CCC confirm Cross's findings: They fear the immediate ego damage of failure. This "fear," however, is more than a product of conditioning, for it does not occur in a social class vacuum. As this chapter has shown, it is also a product of the dialectic between the personal and institutional aspects of class, for the students fear failure not only for its immediate psychological consequences but also for its long-range consequences in terms of identity and life chances. Similarly, in *Boys in White,* Becker and his colleagues describe both immediate and long-range perspectives, defining the latter as "those which have brought the individual into the situation, [specifically the idea] that medical school is a good thing and that it is necessary to finish medical school in order to practice medicine."[13]

The question begs itself: If community college students avoid risk situations and if they are more passive in their approach "to life and its demands," why are they in school at all? The answer lies in the long-range perspective, which, as seen in Chapter 1, primarily concerns notions of "betterment" in this critical juncture in their lives. What Cross does not see is that students' "psychological" lack of self-confidence is more than an artifact of past scholastic performances; it is also a product of the meanings that arise in the interplay of identity, aspirations, institution, and social class. In short, to say training program students simply avoid academic opportunities or academically "risky situations" misses what actually was going on—the attempt to manage and control the dangers and indignities inherent in the school situation.

In one respect this process is similar to that found in the medical school culture. The authors of that study report that

the superiors in a hierarchy may set tasks that subordinates find unmanageable, may create situations in which subordinates feel it necessary to defend themselves or through ignorance of the subordinates' perspective unwittingly do damage to the subordinates' interests. If any of these occur, subordinates may find it necessary to set collective standards.[14]

A crucial difference, however, was that in the medical school the short-range perspective was compatible with the students' long-range interests:

> the long-range perspective that students brought with them has remained and been transformed by the school experience, being made more professional and specific. There is enough congruence between their long-range perspectives and the immediate perspectives they develop in response to the problems school sets for them to allow this kind of transformation to take place. Pedagogically speaking, the worst situation would be that in which there was such disparity between the students' long-range perspective and the immediate perspectives enforced by the situation that no such transformation could take place. In the medical school we studied the situation probably approaches the optimum, for the immediate perspectives students acquire in school, have an effect of the kind the faculty desires on their long-range perspectives.[15]

For the training program students in CCC, the situation probably approached the point of diminishing returns, for their immediate responses to the contingencies of school life had an effect on their long-range perspective neither they nor their teachers desired. By working at cross-purposes with themselves, they were, in effect, ensuring the very defeat they wished to avoid. On those occasions when students expressed an awareness of this dilemma, they lamented their absenteeism and limited effort in a way that seemed to increase the moral responsibility they took for their own sense of inadequacy and frustration.

In the following poignant vignette, an unusually perceptive student comments on this predicament:

> I am sitting alone in the student lounge when Red, a business student, wheels in the TV, connects it to the videotape player and shows "News and Views" [a student-produced videotape announcing school events and presenting interviews of teachers]. Red sits next to me and says, "It's really interesting how apathetic the students are here. This is the sixth week we've been doing 'News and Views' and you and I are the only ones here. It's not as though we didn't put up posters [announcing the time and place of the showing] all over the place." I say that I agree with him, the students are apathetic, but this may not be the best example of it.

Red: "I know what you're going to say; that the attendance thing and the fact that nobody does anything are better examples." He also mentions that the lack of involvement in student government is another indicator of apathy. I ask him why he thinks this is.

Red: "In America now—and the James Bond movies really helped it along—it isn't cool to feel emotionally attached to anything or anybody. Maybe with your family, your girlfriend, or your guy, but it just isn't cool to show any emotional involvement with a school. I've noticed all year that the kids in this school are anti-intellectual and to be honest so am I. And I ask myself why. I think it's because people have a need to pull others down to their level. Working-class people are notorious for this; they love to think that they are better than intellectuals or just plain middle-class people who don't work with their muscles. My father's like that. That's an emotional thing, anger."

Red goes on to say that not only might there be this kind of anger but that the students may resent the teachers because the teachers represent education and intellect. He says that the most popular teachers are the ones who themselves are working-class people. "But there are some teachers who just talk *way* over the heads of their students and they'd have to be really out of it if they didn't know they were doing it." Red says he's heard many students complain about this problem. He then says that maybe one way to get students to watch "News and Views" is to "put something anti-intellectual on."

The show comes around on the tape for the third time. One segment is Red himself interviewing Johnson—one of the most academically oriented teachers in the school. The interview concerns his Western civilization course next semester. Johnson says in a very slow, methodical manner: "A lot of the course is lecture because that's still an important form of communication. But we'll also be making more use of the [video and audio] tape center." In the interview Red asks him what they will be covering.

Johnson: "We'll start with the impact of liberalism, the causes and consequences of the American and French revolutions on our ideology, the scientific revolution, how World War I led to World War II and to the Cold War, and whether the Cold War is really ending. And, I forgot to add, in addition to making use of the tape center where some people who actually acted out history can be heard and seen, we will make more extensive use of our library resources than we were able to first semester."

In the interview Red winces and says: "That sounds like a lot of studying."

Johnson twists his mouth in an effort to turn down a smile and says, "Yes, it will be a lot of studying."

Red turns to me and says, "Did you see my face when he described the course and his smile when I said it would be a lot of studying? That's what turns me off."

HBL: "What does? The description of the course or his smile?"
Red: "Both."
HBL: "How does it turn you off?"
Red: "In a way it's puzzling, because we're here to get a better job, to make something of ourselves, but we put down the school and stay away from it. This teacher gives you a lot of reading and writing to do and immediately you're pissed off. That happened in human relations class, in marketing, and in Tobin's [English] class. It's biting the hand that can feed you. You'd think people would try harder, but they don't and that's bad for them, for me, for anybody."

Although he perceived a relationship between social class and anger, Red, and students like him, believed that as individuals they ideally should attempt to make the best of an unfortunate situation; it was, they believed, their individual responsibility to do so. Yet meeting this responsibility meant meeting the demands, expectations, and values of those who made them feel inferior; and so as a matter of honor it became necessary for students to resist, even if that meant feeling badly about it. They could not completely resolve this contradiction any more than they could erase class distinctions; they could only turn once again to that behavior described here that expressed their frustrations, yet at the same time preserved that modicum of integrity needed to persist.

NOTES

1. Similarly, Becker, Geer, Hughes, and Strauss distinguish between immediate and long-range perspectives and discuss the interplay between them: "Long-range perspectives are those which have brought the individual into the immediate situation: in this case, the would-be medical students' perspectives that medical school is a good thing and that it is necessary to finish medical school in order to practice medicine. Given this perspective, the student enters medical school and, in terms of his long-range perspectives, finds himself faced with a number of specific problems. In the face of these, he develops an immediate short-run perspective. In most of our analyses we are, as we shall see, concerned with the development of short-run situational perspectives and deal with long-range perspectives primarily by way of specifying the conditions under which a given immediate situational perspective comes into being." Howard S. Becker, Blanche Geer, Everett C. Hughes, and Anselm Strauss, *Boys in White: Student Culture in Medical School* (Chicago: University of Chicago Press, 1961), p. 35.

2. For a discussion of a similar problem among working-class adults, see Richard Sennett and Jonathan Cobb, *The Hidden Injuries of Class* (New York: Random House, 1973), Ch. 1, pp. 53–118.

3. Ralph Turner, "Role-Taking: Process Versus Conformity," in *Human Behavior and Social Process: An Interactionist Approach,* ed. Arnold M. Rose (Boston: Houghton Mifflin, 1962), p. 23.

4. Turner has commented on this conception of role playing, "The actor is not the occupant of a position for which there is a neat set of rules—a culture or set of norms

—but a person who must act in the perspective supplied in part by his relationship to others whose actions reflect roles that he must identify." Ibid.

5. Stanley Aronowitz, *False Promises: The Shaping of Working Class Consciousness* (New York: McGraw-Hill, 1973), p. 90.

6. Erving Goffman, *Asylums: Essays on the Social Situation of Mental Patients and Other Inmates* (Garden City, N.Y.: Doubleday, 1961), p. 304.

7. Paraphrased from Goffman, ibid., pp. 304–5.

8. Bergen Evans and Cornelia Evans, *Dictionary of Contemporary American Usage* (New York: Random House, 1957), p. 378.

9. Peter Berger and Thomas Luckmann have discussed theoretically the origins and implications of competing definitions of the situation and the precariousness that can follow in *The Social Construction of Reality: A Treatise in the Sociology of Knowledge* (Garden City, N.Y.: Doubleday, 1967), pp. 92–116. Joan Emerson's view of the doctor-patient relationship is theoretically similar to the occurrences in the community college classroom insofar as shifting definitions of the situation complete against each other. See her "Behavior in Private Places: Sustaining Definitions of Reality in Gynecological Examinations," in *Recent Sociology No. 2: Patterns of Communicative Behavior*, ed. Hans Peter Dreitzel (New York: Macmillan, 1970), pp. 74–97.

10. Georg Simmel, "The Web of Group Affiliations," in *Georg Simmel: Conflict and the Web of Group Affiliations*, trans. Kurt H. Wolff and Reinhard Bendix (New York: Free Press, 1964), pp. 163–65.

11. Sennett and Cobb, *The Hidden Injuries of Class*, pp. 97–98. (Emphasis in the original.)

12. K. Patricia Cross, *Beyond the Open Door: New Students to Higher Education* (San Francisco: Jossey-Bass, 1971), pp. 30–31.

13. Becker, Geer, Hughes, and Strauss, *Boys in White*, p. 35.

14. Ibid., p. 312.

15. Ibid., p. 432.

4

TENSION MANAGEMENT AND PERSPECTIVES IN THE COMMUNITY COLLEGE: THE LIBERAL ARTS AND HUMAN SERVICES STUDENTS

Successful completion of the Liberal Arts and Human Services programs required demonstrating both familiarity with abstract concepts and competence in working with them. The students in these curricula associated such intellectual activity with upward mobility, for after graduation they could either transfer to a four-year institution or more easily acquire a white-collar position. It was not that they saw middle-class people as intellectuals, but that working with ideas was seen as necessary to become middle class. This chapter analyzes the perspectives of three groups of liberal arts and human sciences students, each of whom attributed a different meaning to working with ideas and to the upward mobility implied. The three groups are the male students, the female students, and a small group of older students of both sexes.

THE MALE STUDENTS

That the Liberal Arts and Human Services programs signaled a change in social class was clear. When followed by transfer to a four-year college or university, they greatly increased the likelihood in the years ahead of a student's not having to wear boots to work. The Human Services program in particular was designed to produce lower-order white-collar workers who would acquire varying degrees of authority over and responsibility for clients or publics. In the simplest of terms, the males were ambivalent over the prospect of mobility and the "intellectualizing" necessary to make that prospect a reality. There were two reasons for this: To enroll in either curriculum and then do poorly was publicly and privately mortifying and to do very well in either curriculum called for changes in values, lifestyles, and self-images that were socially and personally distressing. Both failure and success, then, left these students vulnerable. First, the consequences of failure will be examined.

Like the training students, the liberal arts and human service students feared the immediate ego consequences of failure. Certainly students in every school and at all levels of education face this same problem, but for community college students with poor academic histories continued failure took on two additional dimensions: First, as discussed earlier, it confirmed and ratified those doubts and fears about one's capacities and worth. Second, it negated the prospect of social mobility to which they had publicly committed themselves. They were, after all, attempting to exit the blue-collar world, and in this sense they had put themselves on the line. Students' awareness of this is seen in these remarks concerning poor academic performance:

Chris: "I really got myself into it this time. He's been talking about the Roman Empire and I don't know what's going on. I got a 42 on my last test. I don't care, I'm going to flunk this one too."
HBL: "You don't care?"
Chris: "No, I know how to drive a truck."
We both smile at Chris's gallows humor.

(a liberal arts student)

I ask George and Mike how their community problems test was. They both say it was difficult and that they did not do all the reading. Mike says that because his grades are so low he is thinking of transferring into law enforcement next semester.
George: "Hey, man, stick with it. They'll help you get through. You're no flunky."
Mike: "Well I flunked the midterm and there's no way I passed this." He discusses the difficulty he is having in his other courses and says he dislikes most of his teachers. Despondently, he says, "At least I gave it a shot. Being a cop ain't so bad. It beats a lot of other things."

(two human services students)

That reaching the end of the rope could be terribly mortifying was evident in a social science class where a student whom I knew to be failing and considering withdrawal complained of the overemphasis on earning a college degree:

Bert: "Why go to school if you're going into a trade? To learn thirteenth-century Shakespeare?"
Greenberg: "Shakespeare didn't write in the thirteenth century."
There is a roar of laughter from the class and comments like, "OK, Bert" and "Good goin'." The two students on either side of him rib him with their elbows.

[After class] I talk with Bert, who is obviously still upset. I am in a quandary, because I don't want to upset him further but I want to know what he's thinking. I ask what I think is a neutral question, knowing that Bert will know what I mean: "What do you think, Bert?"

Bert: "Fuck those guys. I'm no genius, but just because I don't know when Shakespeare ... Shit, if my uncle gets me an apprentice [ship in an electrical worker's union] I think that's OK. That suits me just fine."

HBL: "Ya, but you sound angry about it."

Bert: "I'm just pissed off right now. That was a real put-down."

HBL: "Are you pissed off because of that or because of the whole situation?"

Bert: "It's the whole goddamn thing. ... Everytime you screw up you know you're closer to being out."

[Two days later] I ask Bert if he is going to drop out. He tells me he can't get into the union, they're laying off men now. He says he doesn't know what to do since work is hard to find: "It's really bad —if you fuck up school you just hang it up and kiss it goodbye. That's why I went into liberal arts."

I ask him to explain.

He says, "Because if you make it through all four years you can get a job. You don't have to worry about unions unless you're on top and they're working for you."

On the one hand, becoming a union member suits Bert fine: on the other hand, he'd like to be on top. The other students similarly implied a negative evaluation of their own working-class status. Clearly, it was respectable to be a blue-collar worker, but there was always the notion that it was somehow better to be a white-collar worker because that was evidence of your intelligence, drive, and virtue.[1] As would be expected when people are ambivalent about such an important matter, the students were quite uncomfortable in their predicament.

Compounding this fear of failure and the loss of mobility it implied, these students were also apprehensive about the consequences of success and the mobility it would bring. Again, this "discovery" was a product of the students' views and behavior concerning "intellectual work," for this was the activity they saw as crucial for access to middle-class positions. The first hint of this "fear of success" came during the first week of school when a class of liberal arts students was asked to intellectualize consciously:

Sloan [the teacher] enters the room and on the blackboard writes his name, the name of the course, and the textbook titles. There are 20 males and 6 females in the class. He is wearing a necktie and corduroy sport jacket with elbow patches. He sports a moustache. About 35 years old—academic-looking. It is 3:05—he is waiting for 3:10 [when the bell signals the official beginning of class].

Teacher to class: "If I were Mort Sahl I would keep you amused. But I'm not, so does anyone know any funny stories?"

Student: "Who is Mort Sahl?"

Sloan: "Can anyone tell us who Sahl is?"

There is no response from the class.

Sloan: "Anyone?" Finally, an older woman student (in her 50s) volunteers.

Sloan: "Hmmm. Well maybe second semester I'll tell some of his jokes, there's too much to do this semester. . . . This course will be especially exciting if you are exciting. We won't be belaboring small points here—that may be some comfort to some of you. We will be looking at the big historical picture." He begins his lecture on the importance of studying history. . . . His manner is calm, quiet, relaxed and flowing. . . . After a few minutes he says: "In this course you will organize much of the material yourself using certain key concepts I give you, for example, concerning the ways in which institutions develop." He stresses the importance of taking good notes: "It will be helpful for organizing material for yourself." He asks them to purchase the two books listed on the board: "The Jordon book is a superior piece of writing and will be challenging to you. Your first assignment is to read the preface—it is an excellent essay. . . . Reading is an essential part of this course. Lectures and discussions constitute the second part of this course. Naturally, lectures are open for discussion at any time. . . . Are there any questions?"

Male student: "Is there any kind of booklet which gives the objectives and the units in the course. We got one in biology and —."

Sloan: "No. That's what I was trying to tell you before. Our approach will be conceptual. . . ."

After the students have put their names, majors, and other information on index cards, Sloan introduces himself by name and as "an historian and teacher by profession." [He tells the class which graduate schools he has attended and where he has previously taught. Later he comments:] "There is no school policy concerning attendance. But I think you will be better off if you come to class. If you find the classes dull or a bloody bore and would rather read—OK. Also, I will be glad to supervise independent study. . . . Your first assignment before you read Jordon's preface is to write an intellectual autobiography. Please do not write more than 1,000 words."

There is much laughter from the class—some of it whooping laughter from the males. Sloan looks around as if to discover what it is that is so funny.

Sloan: "Let's make it a maximum of four typed pages." More laughter. He looks confused as he continues: "Some of you have had rich and exciting lives and will write up to four pages, others, not so —maybe you'll write only two or three pages." This is said seriously, with no apparent intent to insult. Much laughter from the class— except for the older woman and one Oriental student.

Student: "What if you don't have a typewriter?" Laughter from the class.

Sloan: "How many don't own a typewriter?" Everybody but the older student raises their hands and there is more laughter.... He explains that what he wants in the intellectual autobiographies are the factors—especially ideas—in their backgrounds that have been most influential in their "intellectual development." Some students have curious expressions on their faces which I take to be amazement or bewilderment: others have smiles which barely fit their faces. The teacher says that in writing the essay they should consider the following questions: "Who are you? Why did you come to college and what do you want out of it? Where are you going and what has made you what you are?"

Student: "Can it be fiction?" Much raucous laughter....

[Near the end of the class] Sloan: "Are there any questions?"

Student: "How much will the books come to?"

When Sloan says 15 dollars the student replies, "Fifteen? That's a lot of bread." Sloan shrugs his shoulders and says the books are worth it....

After class I follow five male students down the stairwell. Some of their comments: "This is a classic case of bad vibes." "He's gotta be kidding asking us to write this." "I'll have to hire a secretary." "How are we going to get rid of him? Shoot him?" "That guy's got a lot of balls—four pages by Thursday." "He's going to be too much—too much work!" "He's a liberal." "And probably a fag." More laughter.

We have read some of their essays in Chapter 1. Despite their protestations, the students did write them. It was, after all, the first week of school and there was some initial enthusiasm. Although none was more than three pages, their essays were serious, and the students were not unaware of the importance of the next two years. Writing an intellectual autobiography, however, was not something they thought they would ever be asked to do, even in school. Indeed, in the essays students referred to the circumstances of their lives rather than crediting ideas, *per se,* in the formation of their consciousnesses or behavior. As the teacher consented to share the essays with me, he remarked that they were "social autobiographies" and not "intellectual" ones. In short, for these students the assignment was as unusual and humorous as asking Harvard women to learn to use a jackhammer.

Asking students to do something they consider unusual can have a pedagogic value, if, to use the same example, Harvard women were asked why they thought learning to use a jackhammer humorous. They would see that it is a violation of traditional sex roles and, furthermore, that it is an activity relegated to those of a different social rank. Such a strategy was not the intention of City Community College teachers, for, as will be seen, most were unfamiliar with the social class milieu, educational levels, and sensibilities of their students. The humorous effect, though, was the same, because, for the male students, being asked to intellectualize was seen as a violation of traditional sex roles and as something people of their station did not do. Harvard women might learn to use a jackhammer in response to a challenge, but for City Community College students, acquiring conceptual knowledge, truly valuing it, and freely using it was a more serious matter, as it also meant acquiring a self-image they did not presently have. This undertaking was no game, no pedagogic trick, and the laughter in the classroom was but one expression of this tension. The more permanent management of this tension gave rise to a perspective that now will be examined, that mediated between this tension and the demands of teachers.

Students occasionally would berate each other for even the appearance of intellectualism:

> I went to the hallway by Leland's room to wait for his class to begin. As an older student (24 or 25) walked by carrying a brief case, Gary and three of his friends were coming from the other direction.
> Gary: "Is that the intellectual with the brief case?"
> Gary put on a British accent as he said this and mimicked a feminine gait. The other three laughed. The older student (who I do not know but have seen in some classes) did not acknowledge them.
> (hallway conversation)

> Clay: "Hey, Tony, tell 'em that word you used in class."
> Tony [to a group of liberal arts students]: "Affront."
> John: "What's it mean?"
> Tony: "An insult."
> John: "Well, let me affront you, Tony, that's a pretty educated word to be usin'."
> Tony: "Up yours." Laughter from the others.
> (conversation in a bar)

Peer pressure could be much more direct:

> Brian really begins to pour out his feelings [in a social sciences course]. He says he really isn't racist, although he goes along with some of his friends' remarks. He says he has done some reading and is beginning to understand his and his friends' feelings. . . .

[Later as I am having coffee with some students] Brian comes over to our table. Steve says: "Here comes Brian. What, did you finish reading another book?"

Brian: "What do you mean?"

Steve: "All that shit you gave Mr. Langley about lovin' the bunnies and readin'. You didn't read shit."

Brian: "That was for Mr. Langley's benefit."

[Still later when Brian and I are alone] Brian says he really did do some reading. He reaches in his green bag and shows me a copy of *The Negro in American History.* I ask why he just doesn't ignore Bill and Tom.

Brian: "I don't know. I grew up with them. The only reason I told you was because I thought you saw me reading it in the library."

I tell him I didn't see him.

Brian: "I don't want to give you the wrong impression. I don't do *that* much reading, but this was really an interesting book."

For Brian to admit publicly that he had read and been influenced by a book that was not even assigned would have been to risk sacrificing membership in his peer group. Ostracism is difficult no matter what the principle involved, but it is especially so for a student not fully confident of sustaining the intellectual performances needed to alter his very identity. In such cases a student is doubly vulnerable— he risks ostracism, yet has no guarantee that his efforts will pay off. This is the case in the following vignette:

Walt: "All this stuff is new to me. In high school all you did in history was dates and places, but Bailey says he doesn't care that much about it so long as we know roughly when something happened. It's really kind of interesting when he explains why things like World War I happened but it's hard to understand. I know what he means when he says it but I can't explain it afterward."

HBL: "Why don't you see him at his desk?"

Walt: "I have—a couple of times."

HBL: "What about asking someone in the class?"

Walt: "I've done that too. You know Simmy? She's really smart. Ugly, but smart. I usually talk to her upstairs where John and those guys won't see me."

HBL: "Because she's ugly?"

Walt: "That, and I'd be talking to her about history."

I ask him to explain. Actually, I know what he means but I want to hear it from him.

Walt: "Just before a test you should see how they butter her up, but otherwise they don't care. I think Bailey's the best teacher I ever had. He really makes it interesting."

HBL: "You can't let John know that?"
Walt: "I can say Bailey's alright, but I can't say 'Oh, wow, this is the best course I ever had!' "

(conversation in the lounge)

Taking this as an important datum, I made it a point to talk alone with John:

After a few minutes of social talk I ask John what he thinks of Bailey's class.

John: "Bailey's pretty good. I've never heard a vocabulary like his. He speaks six feet over my head sometimes."
HBL: "Ya, I've heard him lecture. Do you like his lectures?"
John: "You have to read the book to know what he's talking about. Even then it's hard; I got an F and a D on the tests. I thought I'd do better because it's interesting and you pick it up faster."
HBL: "I remember I had a teacher like Bailey once. He was one of the best teachers I ever had."
John: "Ya, Bailey is a little weird, but I'd say he's better than any *history* teacher I had in high school."
HBL: "Do you study much for him?"
John: "No, just to get a C. They say with a C you can transfer, that that's a good college grade."

Despite the impression John has given Walt, John does admit that he reads the history book and that he finds Bailey interesting. Walt's impression is not entirely incorrect, however, as John is limiting his effort by settling for a C. The vulnerability felt by Brian and Walt is not unlike the many anxieties of the *nouveaux riche* or, for that matter, any person whose status changes, for the new status and image produce a variety of problematic situations. Old relations are threatened and may have to be broken, new ones must be established, and one's personal life has to be reordered as one devotes more time to new activities, such as reading and studying. Students like Walt and Brian were criticized not as "grade-busters" or "average raisers," as liberal arts courses were not graded on a curve, but as people who were too quickly shifting from a working-class to a middle-class orientation. One student was quite explicit about this:

Frank tells me Larry is generally disliked by "the guys" even though he used to be part of their group. He complains Larry now studies too much, that he takes school as if it were the "only thing around."
Frank: "He's pushy and always browning the teachers."
HBL: "What do you mean, he's pushy?"

Frank: "He doesn't want to go to U _____ [the state university] he wants to go to _____ or _____ [small private colleges with excellent reputations]. Do you think he can get in there?"

HBL: "I don't know, really."

Frank: "Well if he does, bye-bye Larry. Have a good time."

(conversation in the cafeteria)

Such students were resented (by students in all majors) because in effect they were willing to leave others behind, including their friends. If they were seen as doing too well without seeing anything wrong with that, then they were deserters, they had shown how weak their allegiances were. Of course, students who were doing "too well" did see "something wrong with it," as demonstrated by Brian's and Walt's awareness of the double jeopardy in which they had placed themselves. Their dilemma extended not only to their peers but to their families. Said one student whose father and brother were longshoremen:

Don: "They're glad I'm in college. I'm the baby in the family. But things aren't the same anymore at home. You know, they tease me. They say, 'Do you really want to be a teacher?' Well, I do even if I feel funny about it."

HBL: "What's there to feel funny about?"

Don: "Doing something different. I think I can do it, even if it means taking shit. Maybe they're just jealous, my brothers."

(conversation in the game room)

There is always a price to be paid for emancipation, and in cases like this those who make the move feel ambivalent about their success in school. They have been told of the virtues and dividends of educational achievement, yet they cannot feel completely comfortable with it.[2] Most male students, however, were more circumspect in their level of effort. If a transition was to be made in their lives, it would occur slowly. Having done poorly in high school, it is not surprising that still in their own city and still with old friends, they would proceed tentatively and cautiously. Like the training students, they were hedging against the possibility of failure, yet they were also cushioning themselves from the social-psychological consequences of success, of becoming "middle class."

We have already seen how this concern limited effort, but it also limited attendance. There were, of course, immediate reasons for absence: work, personal problems, boring classes, and so on. As noted, Patricia Cross explains such restrictions as simply a product of expecting failure on the basis of past performance, but it is much more complex than that. Certainly Cross is correct in stating that students take into account past performance and that this causes considerable apprehension; but they also wondered whether the community college might intervene to change their fates, and, in effect, dampen or erase past disappointments. At the risk of overemphasis, their reservations about the consequences of a successful outcome prevented unbridled enthusiasm. As with the restriction of effort, absence also was a mechanism used to manage the pace and uncertainty of crossing a barrier:

> Tim [to a group of students]: "You guys goin' to class?"
> Phil: "Naw, who wants to go to college?" Laughter from the group.
> Tim: "Come on ding-a-ling, let's go."
> Phil: "Sit down and have a beer with the common folk. Don't be uppity; forget about that school shit for a while, will ya?"
> (conversation in a bar, emphasis added)

THE FEMALE STUDENTS

The female liberal arts and human services students were more willing to do assigned work and to participate in class discussions. In most instances they were quicker to respond to teachers' questions and to interject their own thoughts. Most teachers thus thought them better students, not because they were somehow more intelligent but because they were more willing to intellectualize. The following are two representative answers by teachers to the interview question "Do you see any overall differences between your male and female liberal arts and human services students in terms of how they approach their work?"

> I suppose I see the female students as somewhat better—as more willing.... I think part of it is the girls' social climation. They just get used to studying and used to pleasing teachers. And they continue to do that, and teachers like to be pleased and that means entertaining the ideas we work with.
>
> (a female English teacher)

> Maybe I'm exaggerating, but I do think that women are taking more of an advantage of education here. You know the old idea the woman always does better, the girls always did better than the boys, then later the boys did better? And I'm wondering how much of that is social. Seems to be the women were carrying through that old dictum further—carrying it out of the lower school up through the community college.
>
> (a male social science teacher)

Although grading standards varied among teachers, school records revealed that among the liberal arts and human service majors, females as a group outperformed males. Table 4.1 shows that females earned more As and Bs, the same proportion of Cs, and fewer Ds, Fs, and incompletes.*

Many teachers noted that while their female students were better, they still were, in the words of one teacher, "educationally deficient":

> Oh, I think the girls are better than the boys but that's like saying that batting .200 is better than batting .180. The plain, simple fact is that most of these kids—male, female, or neuter—are educationally deficient. Women try harder, they go along with you, they do better than the guys, but compared to students at most senior colleges, no, they don't cut it.
>
> (a math teacher)

The females were less constrained to intellectualize for two reasons. First, they certainly could not be accused of being "fags" as that term was used by the males. They were occasionally accused of being "brainy":

> I saw Jane's term paper, right. She had diagrams with different color pencils and she printed the whole thing. A couple of chicks [in his class] are really cool, but most of them turn me off. It's not just physically, they're too brainy. I wouldn't want to go out with half of them just for that.
>
> (a male student)

Second, female students were less anxious about doing well because they were less anxious about upward mobility. Their allegiance to or sense of honor in their present lifestyles was not as strong and they more readily implied they were after something better:

> Wendy tells me about her job as a cocktail waitress in a local bar. She usually works three days per week, often from 2 P.M. to 2 A.M. This past weekend was the first day she had off in two and a half months. She says she gets very tired, but that it doesn't really interfere with her schoolwork (she's in the Liberal Arts program) because there is little homework. Wendy describes her work: "It is very hard" she says, "to keep up a smile in a bar." She says she has to play several

---

*Failures and incompletes were recorded under the grade of N, "no credit." A student had the option of leaving an N on his or her transcript or of making arrangements with the instructor to pass the course during the following semester.

TABLE 4.1 Percentage of Grade Distribution of Liberal Arts and Human Services Students, by Sex

	A	B	C	D	N*
Female	25	27	19	1	27
Males	12	16	19	9	44
Difference	13	11	0	-8	-17

Note: Read each cell as "of all grades received by females (males) in all their courses, x percent were As (Bs, Cs, and so on)."

Source: U.S. Bureau of the Census, 1970.

roles at once, different roles for different tables. Some people are cheerful, others are not, and your mood has to mesh with theirs. She describes how she has to remember the kinds of moods different people are in so that she can act accordingly with them and that some people expect you to talk with them for a minute or two. She describes some of the criminal types who frequent the downstairs bar. She hates the stench of beer or whiskey on someone's breath. Abruptly she says, "I think I might want to go into drama, and like at this place [the bar] you're always on stage, but then again I might want to teach deaf children too." She describes to me the owners of the bar—the bouncers and the bartenders and the roles she has to play for them. She says it is exhausting work. She adds, "But I do manage to spend a lot of time here (City Community College). It's usually hard to drag myself here, but once I'm here I'm alright." She tells me about the bar where she used to work. "It was much better," she says, "more re- laxed." Poets came in and if it was quiet they would not only read poetry, but everyone would write poetry. Artists would also come in and they would all draw. There were no "animals" in it like there are where she works now.

She has a flower decal on her cleavage, one male student comes by and touches it, another asks where she got it. Afterwards we joke about whether he wants it for himself.

Here's the point of all this. Wendy saw *A Doll's House* at _____ [a university] last week and she has told me her mother encourages her to read books. She has this yearning to see beyond her present everyday world. She also has middle-class career aspirations despite her present situation. Her dress, manner, and speech are all very markedly working class. I think she is in between two worlds.

(conversation in the student lounge)

At one point he [a social science teacher] discusses the great fund of incidental knowledge picked up by city people in the course of their

lives (for example, concerning deviants, ethnic groups). Country people, he states, tend to be very naive when they visit in the city and
they don't know what's going on.

A female student interrupts: "Is that so bad? We don't need all
this trouble and aggravation. Someone comes in from one of the
suburbs and sees a drunk stumbling on the street and says, 'Isn't that
disgusting,' while we don't think anything of it. But they're right. It
is awful."

Two other students state their distaste for life in their part of the
city. Both say they want to get out.

(classroom discussion)

I ask Georgia why she is in the Liberal Arts Program.

Georgia: "What would I do, be in law enforcement? Oh I could
see that in South _____ [her section of the city] with everyone
stealing cars, getting drunk, and popping pills. It was a great place to
grow up, but now it's really gone downhill."

(hallway conversation)

In her studies of women college students, Matina Horner has
stated:

> Women as well as men in this society are immersed in a culture that
> rewards and values achievement and that stresses self-reliance, in-
> dividual freedom, self-realization and the full development of indi-
> vidual resources, including one's intellectual potential.... The
> experimental data ... show that despite the removal for women of
> many legal and educational barriers to achievement, which existed
> until the 20th century, there remains a psychological barrier that is
> considerably more subtle, stubborn and difficult to overcome. I refer
> to this barrier as *the motive to avoid success* [emphasis in the origi-
> nal]. This "fear of success" receives its impetus from the expectancy
> held by women that success in achievement situations will be fol-
> lowed by negative consequences, including social rejection and the
> sense of losing one's femininity.[3]

Horner's conclusions are based on the results of Thematic Apper-
ception Tests (TATs) in which male and female students are asked to
complete a story line concerning various hypothetical educational
achievement of males and females. Reporting the results of a separate
questionnaire study, she has stated:

> The responses on the questionnaire are consistent with performance
> data in suggesting that women ... will not fully explore their intel-
> lectual potential when they are in a competitive setting, especially
> when they are competing against men.[4]

Horner explains her findings as follows:

> The desire to fail comes from some deep psychological conviction that the consequences of failure will be *satisfying*. These girls [I studied] were motivated by the opposite; they were positively anxiety-ridden over the prospect of success. They were not simply eager to fail and have done with it; they seemed to be in a state of anxious conflict over what would happen if they succeeded. It was almost as though this conflict was inhibiting their capacity for achievement.[5]

Horner's subjects were freshmen and sophomores at the University of Michigan, Harvard, Radcliffe, and an unidentified "outstanding Eastern women's college."[6] At working-class and lower-middle-class CCC, Horner's findings seem to be reversed. Unlike the females she studied, the women of CCC seemed more concerned over what would happen should they fail. While they may not have explored their "full intellectual potential," intellectualizing was seen as both a means to and a mark of middle-class respectability, whether by acquiring a job or a husband they otherwise would not have. In reference to academic achievement, social class was a more central concern than gender.[7] Unlike the males Horner studied, the boys of CCC, as discussed above, were more anxious over the social penalties of success.

In summary, change the social class of the institution and it is the males who "fear success" for the social rejection and loss of masculinity it might bring. Taking "fear of success" as an ideal-type construct, with its connotations of intellectualizing and mobility firmly in mind, Figure 4.1 conceptualizes the differences between distinctly working-class and distinctly middle-class institutions.

FIGURE 4.1 "Fear of Success," by Sex and Type of College

		Females	Males
	Elite Universities	+	−
"Fear of Success"			
	City Community College	−	+

THE OLDER STUDENTS

Older students are defined here as those in or beyond their mid-twenties. (Seventy-one liberal arts and human services students were 25 years old and older. Also included here are the older vocational students.) Having already spent several years in blue-collar or lower-white-collar jobs they did not like, they were especially aware that their community college studies could be a critical turning point in their lives. As the telephone repairman said in Chapter 1, he knew it was time to "make a break." Furthermore, believing in their own capacities to develop themselves, those with blue-collar jobs were particularly troubled by the low status and menial nature of their work.

During our conversation he told me that after high school he was in the Marines for three years and then worked for the transit authority for three more years. He told me how hard it was to get into the Carmen's Union and spoke bitterly of his old job: "For three years all I did was open and close doors. It was a nothing job. *I know I have more in me than that.*" He tells me that a few months ago he went to the Veterans Administration and talked with someone about going into the mental health field. He now wants to go into mental health and is enrolled in the Human Services Program: "They don't put crazy people into cellars anymore, you know. There are a lot of new jobs in mental health now—all kinds of things. *I'm not going to be a bed pan nurse, but work with the mentally ill.*" He tells me how he thinks he has the ability to work with the mentally ill in a meaningful way.

(conversation in the student lounge)

As I grew older, in Jr. High and High School, I found that I cared a lot less about grades and how my marks were going. My time and interest was always spent in my social life, girls, sports, etc. . . . That's the reason I think I'm at City Community now. In High School I was always having "a good time" fooling around with the kids. I wanted more to go out and play basketball, baseball, and go out on dates than to study. If I had studied, I'd be in a four-year school now instead of worrying if I can get into the one I want later. I like the people in it. I'll be able to study here and I know I'll be able to approve [sic] my learning ability.

I suppose it was my parents and my brothers and sisters who urged me to go to college. They were older and they knew that it was better to work with your mind rather than with your hands. I didn't know what they meant until I got a job in construction and another one as a watchman. Now I realize the need for a good education.

(from a student's essay)

> By attending college I will learn to improve myself as a person and becoming aware of people around me. I have been out of high school for six years and have found that good job opportunities are limited.
>
> (from a student's essay)

> I hope that City Community College will help me find my true profession. I have worked for too many years at meaningless jobs.
>
> (from a student's oral report)

Another student attended a vocational high school and after graduation worked with his father and brother in an auto body shop. After the death of his father he was employed in another body shop for several years. He concluded:

> Tony: "There wasn't that much to it. You can master something like that pretty fast. I just got sick of working in cold, damp garages." He applied here late and was accepted the day classes began. He wants to go to _____ College. I ask how he is doing in his school work and he replies, "I'll be getting 5 As. I've been working right along. I've been lucky. I found a small group that is really working." His group consists of older students, which, he says, "is good in another way. It's embarrassing to walk by yourself through the cafeteria when it's crowded with teenagers." After discussing the people in his group he says that they are more certain of their abilities than the younger students.
>
> (conversation in an automobile)

Older students with lower-white-collar jobs were also concerned with self-development. The common theme in their comments is that education would provide more freedom and dignity than possible in their old work. They wanted access to "better" roles for the greater freedom these provide in dealing with others and for the dignity and sense of worth that flow from that autonomy:[8]

> Becky tells me that she was strapped in a 9-to-5 mundane job since she graduated high school. She complains that as a secretary she had "no more insight into people than the girl next to me." She describes her job setting—several rows of typists and clerks. She had some minor administrative duties. There was so little possibility of promotion that she decided to come back to school in order to get a job with more responsibility.
>
> (conversation in a hallway)

> In my senior year [of high school] I found myself with the ability to read books and judge them fairly objectively whether I personally liked them or not. I couldn't find anyone to teach me Italian so I began teaching myself. My course in urban life was unsatisfactory, so I

stocked up on pocket guides and began to investigate my own neighborhood. I feel that my interests outside of the classroom have benefited me a great deal. Unfortunately, I did not go on to college but have worked at two very boring, tedious desk jobs for _____ and _____ [two large insurance companies]. So now I am in college. I came with the attitude that I would be able to learn in spite of "bad" teachers. (Please do not take this personally as I do not think you are bad at all!) I am majoring in liberal arts to become a history teacher. That I am sure will make more use of my brains and humanity than my seven years working in the insurance industry.

(from a student's essay)

I entered the business world and worked behind a desk for one year and three months. The meaningless paper work along with the dull atmosphere swallowed me more everyday.

I decided to continue my education. But, my scattered background of high school subjects left me with a small choice. I was accepted to a junior business college in a Medical Secretary course. In a short time I noticed something was wrong. Students in the business course would talk about their business ideas to my half closed ears and constant grin. One would think that I would have looked somewhere else after the unhappy office experience, but I finished the course hoping my new job would be better. It was—for about six months and then it too began to swallow me. I have come back to school so I can find work which will allow me to work less on paper and more on people.

(from a student's essay)

About this time, I became in the legal sense of the word, an adult, and taking full advantage of the freedom I had waited for, moved to a house some friends were renting.

I took on a job as a receptionist. Routine became a part of my life, routine seemed a fair bargain for calling my life my life. But the routine continued and continued and I met the dulled veterans and prisoners of this life daily on the trains and buses and would myself have been dulled had I not been equally stunned. I felt threatened and did all within my power to break it. I traveled a bit. I changed jobs. I began working at a bookstore nights, afternoons, mornings, adhering to any but a nine to five schedule and avoiding all trains and buses. The bookstore was far more intellectually stimulating than any other job I'd held previously. I was well exposed to books but not well read. Most of the people I worked with were a good seven to eight years older and far more well read than I. I felt stifled, but challenged, and have returned to school to read, study and think. While I have no specific career plan I do know that the next job I have will not be a numbing succession of routines.

(from a student's essay)

> Ann: I was very unhappy [being an airline stewardess]. The glamor wears off in a few weeks. It could still be fun, but it dawned on me one day that all I was doing in life was earning a paycheck.
>
> (conversation in an empty classroom)

> Paul: I found work at an employment agency but had a running feud with the boss until finally he said, "If you don't want to do things my way, why don't you leave." So I left. He wanted me to do things a certain way even though I told him it was wrong. Anyhow, here I was 25 years old and I realized I hadn't done much of anything in my life. I wanted to find something I could get *into* and be my own man. . . . So I decided to take up psychology.
>
> (from an informal interview)

The unabashed desires of this group of students to escape the festering powerlessness, frustration, and undistinctiveness of their working lives allowed them, even prompted them, to intellectualize. Doing well in school and playing by the teachers' rules and values were important not just for the economic value of a better job but for cultivating their personal qualities; in this way the idea of personal worth enhanced the worth of working with ideas. Because these students linked class (as reflected in one's occupation) and character, it is not surprising that they viewed most younger students as lazy, irresponsible, or dull:

> Harold: Most of the kids here are not too bright and even the ones who are don't work very hard. It's just a place for them to hang out. They moved the street corner indoors.
>
> (conversation in the cafeteria)

> She claims she feels very much out of place here because she really wants an education: "I remember when I was in high school we took some books home. I hardly ever see the kids here doing that. Maybe it's just the kind of schools they went to, they just weren't taught that you have to work. If I was lazy as that I'd wonder what I was doing in school." There is anger in her voice.
>
> (conversation in the cafeteria)

The differences in the older students' style and level of effort were not only due to their age and job experiences but also to their not knowing other students. Many remained "outsiders" throughout the year and the cliques they did form were more temporary and casual. In short, unlike the younger students, they neither came to school together in the morning nor left together in the afternoon, and this marginality afforded them the freedom to condemn younger students' proscriptions toward academic work. Indeed, the entwining of success, level of effort, and virtue is seen in a school newspaper editorial in which an older student implies that absenteeism is attributable to individual moral weaknesses:

EDITORIAL

ABSENTEEISM

A Crime of Omission

Believe it or not, a college student has certain recognizable responsibilities. The major responsibility is to actually attend college.

I'm not pointing the finger at anyone ... but absenteeism has become a serious problem at City Community College.

It's pretty damned disgusting when you think about it, too. I mean, how many of you would have the opportunity to become more than just working slobs if it weren't for City Community College. Perhaps the problem is that you haven't really thought about it. Too quickly we forget those anxious Summer days when we wondered long and hard about the demanding challenge of college life and whether or not we could meet that challenge.

I have been out of school for fourteen years and maybe I appreciate school more than the average student. Since I never really thought I had the brains or ambition to make a go of it at the college level I'm happy as hell with the progress I've made so far and to the City Community College people in general for the faith they've shown in me.

Jesus Christ kids, wake up! If you flunk out of this school you're up shit's creek without a paddle. You're going to have to get a job. You're going to have to work for a living. And believe me, that's a bummer. I did it for fourteen years, including three in the U.S. Army, and I know. For God's sake and your own don't drop out.

For the author of the editorial, absence was a matter of irresponsibility, of taking college for granted, of failing to act on ambitions; there was, of course, no expressed awareness that he and his cohorts were less socially constrained from playing an idealized version of the role of student. (That their teachers did in fact consider them ideal students is discussed in Chapter 5.)

A final note on the liberal arts and human services students—regardless of age, social class was an important concern for them, but the greater congruence between their needs and aspirations and those of their teachers militated against the episodic open conflict described in Chapter 3.

Conflict or resistance is, of course, to be expected in most schools, for as stated by Willard Waller:

The teacher-pupil relationship is a form of institutionalized dominance and subordination. Teacher and pupil confront each other in the school with an original conflict of desires, and however much that conflict may be reduced in amount or however much it may be hidden, it still remains.[9]

To recapitulate, the data indicate that for most City Community College students, it was not just role set subordination but social class subordination as well that gave substance to the "conflict of desires." Returning now to the teachers and their responses to the students, we round out our examination of the inner life of the school.

NOTES

1. For an analysis of this phenomenon, see C. Wright Mills, *White Collar: The American Middle Classes* (New York: Oxford University Press, 1956), pp. 200–5.

2. While Burton Clark described the process of "cooling-out" community college students, that is, of weeding out unpromising students, he did not adequately recognize the great difficulties of "warming up" in a community college. Burton Clark, "The 'Cooling-Out' Function in Higher Education," *American Journal of Sociology* 65 (May 1960): 269–76.

3. Matina S. Horner, "Femininity and Successful Achievement: A Basic Inconsistency," in *Feminine Personality and Conflict,* ed. Judith M. Burdwick et al. (Belmont, Calif.: Wadsworth, 1970), pp. 45–47.

4. Ibid., p. 67.

5. Quoted in Vivian Gornick, "Why Women Fear Success," in *Current Perspectives on Social Problems,* ed. Judson R. Landis (Belmont, Calif.: Wadsworth, 1973), p. 152.

6. Horner, "Femininity and Successful Achievement," p. 63. The reader should note that Horner's techniques, concepts, and findings have been questioned by subsequent research. For a review of this research, see David W. Tresemer, *Fear of Success* (New York: Plenum Press, 1977). Tresemer, however, does *not* include social class homogeneity as a criticism of Horner.

7. It may be as Komarovsky suggests, that after these girls transfer to a four-year school or begin their first job, parental and peer pressures may dampen achievement motivation in favor of marriage. In light of the findings of this report, these pressures in themselves may not be enough, for the mobility of these females would first have to be assured (even if not yet achieved) or clearly denied before plans were changed. Mirra Komarovsky, "Functional Analysis of Sex Roles," *American Sociological Review* 15 (August 1950): 508–16.

8. Richard Sennett and Jonathan Cobb, *The Hidden Injuries of Class* (New York: Random House, 1972), p. 30.

9. Willard Waller, *The Sociology of Teaching* (New York: Wiley, 1932), p. 195.

5
TENSION MANAGEMENT
AND PERSPECTIVES IN
THE COMMUNITY COLLEGE:
THE TEACHERS

THE LIBERAL ARTS AND HUMAN SERVICES TEACHERS

The liberal arts and human services teachers brought with them experiences and occupational identities from other academic settings, the assumptions being made that the educational levels of students and the status, values, and understandings associated with intellectual activity would not be radically different. In the daily life of City Community College, the chief problem for these teachers was to resolve the strains posed by students who challenged the accuracy of those assumptions. More precisely, teachers had to preserve or acceptably modify their identities as intellectual beings in the face of an unreceptive, skeptical audience. The perspectives that evolved were in effect the organized solutions to this dilemma.

That teachers had misjudged the situation is evident in the tape-recorded interviews and in comments made in and out of class:

> Interviewer: Can you describe your expectations of the students compared to what you actually found here?
> Teacher: They were much lower than I expected initially. In one class I dropped all standards.
> Interviewer: Why was that?
> Teacher: Well, the class, I don't know, the class just fell apart. They weren't ready, it turned out. They had no background, and by the time I found out they had no background it was almost already half way through.
>
> (social science teacher)

> Teacher: In the very first semester of my teaching [at another community college in a suburban community] we used _____, which is a very difficult book and I used some other additional material. And it didn't work too badly, because, you know, it was an evening course

where the average age was higher and they were of a greater motivational level, but *even there* I began to realize immediately that this book was much too difficult even for that level, but manageable. And so when we went into the daytime teaching we began to search for material that would be more suitable.

Interviewer: So you did have to change some of your readings?

Teacher: Oh yes, yes, yes. I used the _____ book for the first two semesters *evenings.* And after that we began to search for much more moderate reading at a much more moderate level.

Interviewer: What about your expectations before you came *here* compared with what you actually found here?

Teacher: It was really *much*—there were much greater discrepancies.

Interviewer: Can you describe them?

Teacher: Ya, I expected to find a more sophisticated student.

Interviewer: More sophisticated than the other community college?

Teacher: Ya, I don't know why, but I had that illusion. I was under the illusion that in the city you are going to find a somewhat more sophisticated student . . . where the social problems are batted about and are talked about. No matter what side they finally wound up on, I expected them to be much more aware than they actually were. I found that it's kind of an interesting thing. When you take places like _____, _____, and _____ [sections of the city] what you really have got is not urban students in the sense, you know sometimes we think of urban as *urbane* or something like that—more sophistication—but they're really insular. These are little pockets of insularity. We used to think of rural people as rubes who are very unsophisticated, and insular in many, many ways. Because they're in that little community which gives them something and denies them something.

(a social science teacher)

Interviewer: Did you at any point in the year have to revise your courses? For example, decrease the amount of reading or increase the length of time you gave them to read something?

Teacher: Ya, ya. I had to. My total experience was to slow down. I had to . . . uh . . . it's very hard to know the pace, but it's a very slow reading pace they have . . . you know. And that is a lesson I had to learn. . . .

Interviewer: Do they give you feedback sometimes when you give them too much work? For example, you said you slowed down, did you slow down because they were telling you that it was too much?

Teacher: Well, I slowed down of course partly because some of them, a good chunk of them, weren't reading at all.

(an English teacher)

Interviewer: I'm interested in comparing your expectations before you came here with what you actually found here. Were there any discrepancies?

Teacher: The thing that was most *shocking* about the year I was here was the first semester . . . was to deal with students to whom the concept of college was alien, to deal with students who *really didn't* understand what college was all about, to deal with students who didn't just apply high school standards to what was going on, but applied poor high school—lower level high school standards—to what was going on. That I think was the real shock. I anticipated that the student would be much more motivated, that they would recognize the opportunity that the school offered. And the first shock was to find that he wasn't ready.

Interviewer: Did you find yourself during the course of the year lowering your standards?

Teacher: Oh, I definitely did. I think I had to. I had to . . . it was the first time I was presented with the idea that it was my responsibility to teach history to students who did not, who could not, read.

(a history teacher)

Teacher: Sometimes they make life a little difficult and they come in not having read the chapter that was assigned for the week, not even having tried the homework. Then I usually just go back, give a brief lecture, and then we talk our way through the chapter. Sometimes most of them come in unprepared.

Interviewer: Does that happen frequently, that they come in unprepared?

Teacher: Yes. In other words you are supposed to read the chapter before you come. Some of them come in and listen to the lecture without having read the chapter. You are supposed to attempt the homework problem beforehand. If you can't do it, you can't do it. They come in and they haven't even looked at it.

(a math teacher)

Interviewer: I'm interested in comparing your expectations before you actually began this job compared with what you actually found here. Were there any discrepancies?

Teacher: Ya, during the course of the first semester I found that a rather disconcerting [long pause] low level of ability in students which I had anticipated there would be some of; but the way it hit me, it came across as a much greater problem than I anticipated. Those kinds of things are disconcerting and I think that when one makes an initial contact with them he's a little hard-pressed to wonder whether his own impressions of what's going on in the world are really so benighted that he's missed the point of what the school is about or what the student generation is about. I'm modest enough to think that I don't have all the answers and so when something like this comes up I'm seriously interested in kind of exploring to see how I could have been so mistaken.

(a history teacher)

Casey [a science teacher] tells me she has classes in which students "just sit and say and do nothing. They're just dead-heads." She says that they are less mature and not as bright as the average high school student. She claims, "They are just not willing to work." She tells me they skip classes frequently and do not do the readings. In one section all of her students are flunking except for one or two Ds. "What a surprise this experience has been for me."

(conversation in an empty classroom)

Craig [a humanities teacher] tells me he was depressed about the absenteeism until he heard that this was happening in other people's courses too. In one of his classes fewer than half are in attendance on any given day. He says, "You know, they pass in no homework, don't take the tests, and don't show up for class. I never expected this."

(conversation in the faculty lounge)

At one point she uses the phrase "battery of tests." Some students have quizzical looks; she asks how many are familiar with the phrase. None of them is. She says it means "a bunch of tests." She is a bit perplexed, but has a slight grin on her face; she appears to be both surprised and amused that they do not know this phrase. Later she uses the word "manifestation," and asks if anyone knows the word; no one does. The same thing happens with "identity crisis." She had used these words several times before realizing that the class was unfamiliar with them. It happens again with "tracking systems" (in reference to education). On the way out she brushes by me and says, "Whew! You never know."

(a social science class)

Robertson [the teacher] is discussing why it is important to study history. He mentions such things as learning from past mistakes, learning about self-identity by placing oneself in an historical epoch, and learning to cope with various interpretations of the past. He asks different students why they think it's important. One student says, "It's confusing to know that certain wars were fought, like the Spanish-American War, the Civil War, and World War I and not to know which one came first or second." Robertson is obviously taken aback. He says, very haltingly, "Ya, those things are important."

(a history class)

Turner [a social science teacher] turns to me and says in a manner that indicates that this is sensitive material: "After the first exam first semester I was shocked by the students' performances—it was so bad. That was a real eye-opener for me. For the rest of the semester we argued about all kinds of things—whether the tests would be multiple choice, true or false, or essay, when the tests should be given, how many tests there should be, the manner in which things should be presented, things like that. This was a very difficult period for me." He adds that he is still shocked by the students' "unawareness." He says that today he asked his class how many had articulated a political philosophy for themselves to that they could identify themselves as being conservative, liberal, Democrat, Republican, and so on. Only two students raised their hands.

(conversation in the cafeteria)

Lewis [an English teacher] tells me he has changed his course for second semester, that it will be considerably easier. I ask why he has done this. "In order to survive," he says.

(conversation in the faculty lounge)

Survival required more than realistically adjusting the amount and difficulty of course work, for teachers needed both an explanation to account for the academic abilities and behavior of their students and a solution that preserved their own morale and professional identity. Everett Hughes has stated:

Part of the problem of academic morale in this country arises from the fact that young men must leave stimulating colleges and graduate schools to teach in less stimulating places. . . . This brings me to the problem of self image. A self-image has a number of facets. It includes one's notion of who one's true colleagues are, the league one's institution plays in, one's notions of one's students. . . . Our problem is not to increase everybody's morale by direct means, although that's a good enough objective. Our real problem is to increase the number of places where faculty can have good morale. I think this can be done, but it will take much ingenuity.[1]

As discussed in Chapter 2, community colleges historically have not shown much ingenuity in articulating a clear-cut mandate and institutional identity to distinguish themselves from other schools. Consequently, the teachers of CCC had to rely on their own ingenuity, and their explanations of and solutions for their day-to-day difficulties with students unavoidably reflected ideological beliefs about the relationship between the individual and society.[2] Their perspectives here are called the conservative, liberal, and radical.

The Conservative Perspective

Four of the 28 liberal arts and human services teachers interviewed attributed students' problems to weaknesses in character or mind. (One was a science teacher, the second English, the third math, and the fourth history.) This view was similar to that of students in that contextual effects were thought to have little importance and individuals were solely responsible for their fates. Given this view, it is not surprising that in this group were the only three teachers who did not decrease the amount or difficulty of their course work. For these teachers the mass of students were to rise or fall on individual merit without any extraordinary teacher intervention. The following is an example of the conservative explanation and solution:

> The students here turn off more easily than I was used to [in other teaching experiences]. In other words if they decide they can't do it they just say the hell with it. It's also the sense of they have to do it and it's hard work to achieve in any area. In other words, this isn't specific to academic discipline but it applies to life in general. If they are going to achieve they are going to have some moments of hard work and digging in. If they have a history of laziness then they'll reap the consequences.... [Later] Actually my standards remained the same throughout the year. If anything, my courses were harder second semester. I felt that if they were going to work, to do anything that amounted to anything, then a little coercion was in order. I told them the first day of second semester, "You either sink or swim in this course."
>
> (a science teacher)

While not oblivious to the relationship between social class and academic performance, conservative teachers emphasized the primacy of an intervening variable—virtue. In the preceding example the teacher felt obliged to coerce "lazy" students; in the following example, the same teacher infers that working-class students, if not morally inferior, are at least uncomfortably "different":

> It's not easy for me to relate to them as people. If I met them on the street or any place else the problem would still exist. There is a gap between the intellectual academic community and the way that they operate. You see that every day.... Nobody tells them to cut a class or to not read a book.
>
> (a science teacher)

The conservative teachers' solution to the problem of professional integrity was to concentrate on their best students. When asked if this was contrary to the idea that the community college should provide an opportunity for disadvantaged or untalented students, their reply was that that was rhetoric:

I don't think we really do help students who never have done well. There's no way that in two years we can turn him around. If a kid has talent but it hasn't been brought out, OK, give him the opportunity to bring that out. But if a kid doesn't have it, I can't give it to him, you can't give it to him, _____ [the president of the school] can't give it to him. He eventually leaves and hopefully just realizes college wasn't for him. I don't worry about him because he's probably right, it wasn't [for him]. To me that's an important job we have to do. It hurts, it's painful, I don't enjoy it, but it happens. The saving grace is the really bright kid. You work with him, you bring him along, you see his progress, you just know he's bright right along the line. Those are rarities, but you get them. There always seems to be one or two every semester. He's the one we're here for.

(a math teacher)

The Liberal Perspective

For 19 of the 28 liberal arts and human services teachers interviewed, the "student problem" was seen as part of a social problem. In interviews and informal conversations, student performance was explained as a consequence of poor inner-city high schools, the low value placed on education, and the absence of a college tradition in working-class families. The following represent this view:

The solid middle-class family generally has some ties and expectations for their children—built-in motivations that they're either going along with or rebelling against, but nonetheless, the whole idea of college education as a means of getting ahead is inculcated in middle-class values and not in the group we're working with.

(an English teacher)

Teacher: I think I didn't quite anticipate what I call morale problems among the students. Their absenteeism is greater than I expected and they have a lot more difficulty tuning in.
Interviewer: What do you think that might be attributed to?
Teacher: I think probably to lousy high schools, a lot of previous failures, low self-esteem—all the things that go along with being raised in their class culture.

(a social science teacher)

No one in their families has gone to college, nor have hardly any of their friends. They haven't had a vicarious college experience. Most of us assumed that they had some field of experience to place this in. We were talking on the basis of our experiences in college, but I think we may have been wrong in that.

(a history teacher)

I'm sure their high schools have a lot to do with the difficulties they're having. They just were not handed the same opportunities that are given to a kid from say _____ or _____ [two affluent suburbs]. I still have difficulty realizing how many of them have gone all the way through high school without being exposed to more than just rudimentary scientific ideas. . . . Maybe they were exposed but the teaching *had* to be inadequate. They were just written off, and that's wrong, so it's no surprise they act the way they do.

(a science teacher)

The solution of these teachers was to attempt to change students' values and conduct, and in this respect, as with liberal social thought in general, they believed in the power and duty of the school to intervene in the lives of students to compensate for social injustices. Although stressing the provision of chances for students to develop themselves in order to find a meaningful place in society, it is important to note that these teachers directly or indirectly stated that students were to be "helped" so long as the social order was not upset:

Interviewer: What about an ideal conception of success in teaching here? Ideally, what kind of successes would you like?

Teacher: OK, I think one job of the community college is to enrich the community by providing vocational jobs which would enrich it economically and by giving back to the community people who are just a little bit more capable of filling community needs; so that we send people back to _____ [name of city] with an understanding of what the issues are, or what to ask of the candidates running for office, or why it's a good idea to help the policeman on the beat, or what the taxes paid for, or what they should ask for their children in the way of child care, of health care or school care. And I think we're capable of doing that.

Interviewer: Some people think that community colleges exist to somehow change the status quo, to intervene in the lives of the students, to somehow change the social order. . . .

Teacher: I know what you're saying, and this is the business that the schools have gone through in the last 20 years when they tried to make a better world, but that better world—civil rights legislation—that better world, not much of that came out of the schools. Whether that's the role of the school I'm not sure, because that presumes then that the teacher has this gift from God of knowing what's right—of rectitude.

(a history teacher)

Teacher: I'm sure you've seen that there are lots of problems here. There are a lot of problems when you get this low. I'm coming more and more to believe that at least now it's not so important to get across a body of knowledge as to get the students to be receptive to learning. That's one-half the battle. My liberal arts students, I try every trick I know to pique their curiosity, to get them to ask a question, analyze a book to see what the author is really saying about the world through his story. It's not how well they do it, it's getting them to do it at all. If I can get them to do it then maybe I can open up something else for them.

    Interviewer: What is the "something else"?

    Teacher: Seeing beyond themselves and their neighborhoods. If they transfer to a senior college and can take that wider view and be successful in their courses I think they will be happier people and better, more productive citizens. They'll be able to contribute something to the system and because of that, to themselves.

(an English teacher)

I do not think that the primary purpose of the community college is to get these kids ready to get a job. I think that that is a secondary purpose, but an important one. But I think that the primary purpose is to prepare them to be willing to take a job and to work with it, but not as an end in itself. . . . You want them to be somehow able to cope with the culture and the society structure as it is without being totally frustrated. . . . That takes a great deal more individual attention in the two-year college than there is in the typical four-year college. Attention given to the individual student. I think that's the crux of it. I don't care how you do it.

(an English teacher)

How did the liberally oriented teachers attend to their students? There were two approaches: lessening the difficulty of course work while simultaneously inflating grades and counseling. Both responses had the dual function of promoting what teachers thought were students' best interests at the same time that they safeguarded the status of intellectualism so central to their own (the teachers') self-images. The ideological rationale for decreasing the quantity and level of course work was that without at least a temporary period of moderation the school could not alter students' lives. Reported one teacher:

As I said, I expected them to work harder to achieve what perhaps they missed at a younger age. [After a while] I realized this may have been unrealistic on my part, in a sense that if they didn't get it in high school they can't change overnight. . . . To keep the standards up there made no sense; for heaven's sake you've got to do it this way [lower the standards].

(a science teacher)

That "doing it this way" had a psychological function for teachers is evident in these two teachers' explanations of how they felt about diluting their courses:

> When you get a class that is very difficult to deal with, you feel extremely . . . you feel threatened in a sense; in the sense that it's kind of a threat to your, well it's an ego threat! You want to get across to them, you want to hopefully help them to deal with certain things in their lives and if you come across a blank wall, what do you do? Well, you know, I tend to *try* to break them through their apathy in some way and it works with some and it doesn't work with others. You just try. You're forced to modify. You're forced to modify. But nonetheless, I try not to give up the notion that we deal with ideas. And even though I have to modify I still try to deal with that.
>
> (a social science teacher)

> The longest part of my work is not teaching _____ [academic area]; it's getting people willing to learn _____ [academic area]. I guess that's a little intellectual gimmick that allowed me to still feel good about what I do. Otherwise I'd be a failure.
>
> (a social science teacher)

Giving higher grades than earned also served the dual function of benefiting both students and teachers. First, higher grades were presumed to be an incentive to students and to facilitate changes in their self-images.

> I'm grading high. I've established a grading system to grade high on purpose as a motivating factor, motivating and morale, and give the students who might get discouraged by flunking immediately or thinking he's going to, to realize that they can succeed and then tightening up standards as much as you can in regard to each individual as they progress.
>
> Interviewer: You tighten standards as you progress?
>
> Teacher: A little bit. But the way I'm grading is still so that a C student could get an A.
>
> (an English teacher)

> It's a bitch! Grading is horrendous. It's a horrendous problem.
>
> Interviewer: What kinds of difficulties are there?
>
> Teacher: I don't like to give objective exams because I think that no matter how minimal their effort is I think a subjective exam is better for them. You know—to make *some* kind of an effort no matter how modest and recording their ideas or how they grasp the ideas we're talking about. And *that,* because of their limited communications skills, becomes quite difficult. So how the hell do you grade?

You do your best.... I don't know whether this is a personal thing or what [but] I find myself being quite lenient with the lower end of the scale. In other words, I hesitate very much to flunk someone if they've made any kind of effort at all.

Interviewer: Is there any particular reason for that?

Teacher: OK, how do I rationalize that? Because I'm being very honest with you. I do rationalize this.... It's kind of a peculiar thing, but I kind of say to myself, "Well, look ... if it was going to be injurious to them and the school they do [transfer] to, to be given an inflated grade, then I wouldn't want to do that ... but if I give a low grade I might eliminate them prematurely." You have to retain some standards, but if school is a place for people to grow, then you have to allow for early mistakes, for that initial poor performance and the poor education they got in their high schools.... But if I know that they're going to finish a two-year program and then go out and get a job, then I say, "Well, look, they've gotten *something* out of this course, they've gotten *something* out of it." And I don't feel justified in hurting them [with a low grade] when *really* in real life, it's not going to really make that much difference.

(a social science teacher)

I will give a C to a D student who is trying and to whom I think a C might possibly be enough incentive to bring them back again. I look on the grade as an incentive, I look on it as a reward for trying hard. I look on it as maybe the thing that will make it possible for the youngster to come back next year.

(a history teacher)

You want to encourage the students. Here you have a student probably from a family who's never gone to college, probably not knowing what is expected of him, and so on.... You don't want to discourage that student right away and yet on the other hand you have a responsibility ... to give honest grades so that if they do transfer they don't get a rude shock and so that after a few years the institutions to which we transfer them do take us seriously and know that our grades mean something....

Interviewer: How do you resolve this?

Teacher: I take a good hard look at the student and if I think he has the potential but has yet to come around I'll give him a break. In the case of kids in the vocational courses I'll give them a C or D when I could give them a D or an F on the assumption that there's no harm done and so the kids can at least get their credit.

(a math teacher)

Inflating grades benefited teachers because, in Gustav Ichheiser's threefold definition of success, they were still producing "valued achievements" in the intellectual arena; the results of these achievements, however, were seen by teachers as lying in the future rather than in immediate classroom rewards. A further indication of the importance of future success is seen in teachers' responses to the question "How do you define success in teaching at a community college such as this one?" Seven of the liberally oriented teachers recounted stories of past students in other community colleges who had become successes; four of these stories were of students who had become teachers. The following are representative examples:

> The very first week [at another community college] I found a couple of students who were far above the rest, and took one of them out of class and, you know, if he wanted to, I encouraged him of course, and immediately began to meet once a week.... This is a guy, who it turned out had flunked out of _____ University and gone into the Army for two years and now he was back.... He now has gotten his Ph.D. and finally ended up at _____ University.... But there were several students like that who we identified who went on to various graduate schools.
>
> (a social science teacher)

> Have you time for me to tell you a marvelous story? This was from the first year in _____ Community College. We had a girl—this was one that I know of because she told me she had never thought to go to college. Her family was a large family and they didn't believe in sending girls to college, and she came to the community college. It opened that year and it was there. She thought she'd get a two-year business degree. So first she was never going to college, then a business degree; she was identified as outstanding, sent into the calculus without having the prerequisites, made an A, made As in _____ [other courses] and went on to the University of _____, and graduated with a B.A. in math. She didn't graduate with As—let's face it —the University of _____ isn't quite the same [as a community college], but there she was with a B.A. where she never would have gone to college at all, let alone thought about transferring to a place like the University of _____, let alone in math, without community college.
>
> (a math teacher)

> Success isn't absolute. Let us say that its most thrilling aspect is those few students who occasionally come to you in a year or two. Oh, let me give you one example. A kid comes to _____ Community College and took a couple of courses with me. The kid was *rough,* but willing and motivated; his language was very unsophisticated, but he was a very sincere kid. Well, I got a call from him a little while ago. He came down to the house. We talked. He's transferred, he's going to the University of _____. He wants to become a teacher; he wants

to teach at the junior high school level, which is the toughest level, and he's going to be *damn good* at it. And he's become from an unsophisticated, a really sophisticated person—a young sophisticate. And I've had this happen a couple of times. And I know it's happened, you know, a minority of the time. That's the ultimate, the best.

(a social science teacher)

Despite the rhetoric that community colleges are "democratizing" institutions, the preceding remarks indicate that even liberally oriented teachers concentrate on their better students. According to Christopher Jencks and David Riesman:

Students [in two-year colleges] are being prepared to transfer on somebody else's terms, and this means that whatever their missionary impulses, instructors must toe a line drawn by somebody else so they concentrate their attention on students whom these outsiders [senior college professors and administrators] regard as worth educating, not on those whom their own ideology puts at center stage. Under these circumstances the community colleges' "open door" policy is valuable for the handful of "late bloomers" who do better academic work than their high school record implied they would. It is not very helpful to the majority whose high school records are an all-too-accurate indication of academic incompetence or indifference.[3]

Although "missionary impulses" and liberal ideology were displaced, it was not only due to pressures from senior institutions; also important was the sense of professional identity and pride teachers received from cultivating a promising student. Said one teacher:

I think the most satisfying kind of student for the community college teacher is the student who never intended to go to college, never felt that he or she had the academic ability or never had the financial resources or whatever, came to the community college more or less because it was there, and found himself or herself, and found a field of study, be it career or transfer, and then went on and made a future from nothing. I've had students like that that found their opportunity, found themselves in the community college, and this is tremendously satisfying. One student like that can make up for 100 of another kind, but it does not happen that often that I know.

(a math teacher)

When asked to reconcile their attraction to the few highly capable students with their belief in aiding the larger number of students, these teachers replied as the other liberally oriented teachers had initially responded: Less able students afforded different but still important opportunities for success. In the following quotes, teachers claim that most students at least got "something" from their courses. Their replies were strikingly similar in that each teacher emphasized the word "something" as if the "something" was indeed not very much at all. This was taken as an indication that they were unconvinced of their own rationale, a theme to which we will return at the end of this chapter:

> I think that the student that shows some obvious academic difficulties or past failures, but seems to be latching on to *something,* seems to be having his curiosity stimulated and seems to be showing some growth is very, very rewarding.
>
> (a science teacher)

> By my criterion if a student struggled and got *some* of the information out of the course I would be pleased. It's terribly difficult for most of them to learn easily, but when you sense they get *something* out of it, then I feel I'm doing something for them too.
>
> (a history teacher)

> I derive a great deal of satisfaction when I walk out of a class and I know that *something's* happened, that there's been some kind of a high. It doesn't happen very often, but occasionally it happens, every once in a while it happens. That's one kind of satisfaction which doesn't happen here [pause] terribly often.
>
> (an English teacher)

> I suppose it has to be that if I can see myself getting across *some* basic concept to these kids, because most of these kids—it's a real challenge —lots of them it's their first experience in science at all. If I can just keep those kids from at least not getting turned off, I can get an awful lot of satisfaction from these kids.
>
> (a science teacher)

> I've had students come to me from time to time—now this is a much simpler level—much less sophisticated level than that minority [of outstanding students]. But I've had a number of students come up to me and they'll say something like this: "Mr. _____, did you see the program on TV, "The Primal Man"? That was just what we were talking about. Do you remember we were talking about so and so and so and so?" And you know, that's kind of a good feeling because you say, "Well, they got *something.*" And then they say they saw *something* on TV or read *something* in the newspapers and they make contact with it. So that feels good.
>
> (a social science teacher)

There are still rewarding students but they're not the thrill of the student who finds his goal. You have to count the students who, even if they don't quite make the goal they had in mind, or flunk out or drop or don't make any goal, still they must get *something* out of the experience. They can't sit around here for a term or a year and get nothing from it."

(a math teacher)

It is my conviction, and I said this earlier, that we touched a student body *that would not have come inside a college.* Now I suppose people can say, "Well, maybe they weren't supposed to go to college. Maybe these are the people who should be fixing cars or running gas stations." And we touched people to whom the whole concept was alien. You know, I'm convinced that those kids that we met six or seven months ago *had no idea* what they were doing or how they were doing it. If they lived in _____ [an affluent suburb] by the time they were in the ninth grade their counselors would have told them about college. But nobody told these youngsters—at least they were sitting in the back of the hall so far away from it, that they never actually looked on their experience. And that's what we're doing that nobody else in the world is. We're not taking these kids away from _____ or _____ or _____ [three nearby universities] or any-place else. They would not have gone to college at all. I mean to the youngsters at this school it was never an alternative between col-leges. For 99 percent of them it was here or no place. It was City Community or go to work in Woolworth's or join the Army or get married or do any of those other things. So what's satisfying is sitting down with a kid, listening to what he says about himself, talking to him, spending some time with him, getting to know him so maybe he will trust you. Only a few students will do this—will let you do this—but when they do you can help them. Who knows, maybe they'll just no longer settle for Woolworth's. But regardless of what they do, maybe you've just helped them understand themselves bet-ter, maybe you've given them *some* insight that will pay off some-time, somehow. You can't do that in 95 percent of four-year colleges. That's not your purpose.

(a history teacher)

Then there are satisfactions one derives from dealing with students on a one-to-one basis, uh, students who are very ... who have had very serious problems that they're very troubled over or who have very serious hurdles to cross; being able to deal with them on a one-to-one basis and really seeing that *some* change does take place in some of them. Really, I've seen it; and that's extremely satisfying. That may not be an intellectual satisfaction—that's a different kind of satisfaction.

(an English teacher)

On several occasions teachers attempted to reach students by "counseling" an entire class at one time. In the classes of the six teachers who attempted this (four of whom were from the social sciences and two from English), students were asked to discuss and analyze their feelings. In a human relations class, for example, students were asked to spend several class hours making a collage that was to be "a personal statement as to the kind of person you are, how you see yourself, how you feel about yourself." Another teacher often began her classes by asking students to form a circle, hold hands, and relate to the group something "good or warm," or, on other days, something "bad or dark," that happened to them during the previous week. There would follow an analysis of these feelings using simplified concepts from R. D. Laing, Freud, and others about whom students were lectured but had not read. In addition to the communication of academic matter it was clear that these classes were also meant to be therapeutic, the major goal the improvement of self-images, or, in the words of one teacher, "raising the psychoemotional consciousness." Similarly, another teacher distributed the following memorandum to her students:

Midterm Thoughts (Yours and Mine)

Mine: In thinking about the way the course is going and what would be most useful for you, I've rejected my original idea of having you all come up either individually or as groups with paper topics since that task is both too difficult and time consuming. After reaching that conclusion, I began to think about what my goals were in assigning papers besides needing them as resources from which to figure out midterm grades. I realized I'm looking for a chance for each of you to write a statement that addresses itself to your idiosyncratic experiences, allows you to look at those experiences through an intellectual (that is *thoughtful*) framework, and use some creativity in doing so. The following are the questions which I suggest as lending themselves to such a paper. If you choose to write on a different topic consider how it addresses itself to these issues and speak to me about it *first*.

Yours: Address yourself in five typewritten pages (NOTE: this is a guideline—if you can say what you want to say more concisely please do so; if you feel that what you need to say needs more space, check yourself out to make sure it's relevant material) to any one of these questions, due on November 2. This is one of those times when organization, grammar, spelling, etc. COUNT.

a. How do you get to know yourself? Compare these forms: looking at your dreams, watching your own behavior, through conversations or other interactions with family or friends, thinking, feeling. Offer observations from a close study of yourself on which you've taken notes during the coming weeks. What conclusions can you draw? You may compare your experience with our discussion of the Freudian model of self.

b. Keep a diary of your feelings over the next couple of weeks. Choose a feeling that recurs frequently (i.e., anger). Examine that feeling. When have you had it before through your life? What features characterize the situations in which it comes up? Why would that be?

c. Do a research paper on someone you know or yourself. Use all possible sources of information especially interviews from family, friends, acquaintances and teachers. You might want to emphasize the comparison between the person's experience of her or himself with others' perceptions of that person. Or, look carefully for chronic feelings and behaviors with an eye to where these came from.

d. Work on the above question looking at a figure about whom you read an autobiography, biography or novel. Consult me first about your choice.

e. Think of a time you wanted to change. Examine why you wanted to and how you went about doing it. What was difficult about it? Did you concentrate on your feelings or behavior? Would you go about it differently now? What conclusions can you draw?

f. Read _____ [name of book] and examine it in light of these questions: How does it relate to your life? What does it say about how a person's world view is formed? About changing a personality?

g. Draw a diagram or picture of either your self conception or your theory of personality. Explain it.

The same liberal social philosophy and counseling strategy was used by the chairman of the business department, whose unusual career path was described in Chapter 2. Three months after school began, this self-avowed "liberal Protestant [minister] who was out to reform the world" or at least "help shape society," instituted a Self-Awareness Workshop for business students. He explained it this way:

> If a person doesn't do anything in accounting, for instance, we recommend that he just forget about that for the semester and come into a personal growth type of thing.... We can't breathe for people: we can't choose for them, but we can do everything we possibly can do to enhance their self-image of themselves, and I think that's the beginning of the educational voyage. I don't want to compromise the academic and I think those that see how I operate know that I won't compromise, but after all, if their self-image, their understanding,

their sense of dealing with themselves is so inadequate that they can't approach the academic, you're crazy to think you can drag in the whole of academic subject matter. So I would try to operate in those areas and I feel quite a sense of mission about it. Academic success is important, but equally important, and if I had to put one before the other, it would be success in helping the student build his own *self-confidence* [his emphasis]. I think the educational system in general turns people off and puts them down and it ought to turn them on, and so self-confidence and self-image is the most important thing that we can do.

Another formal counseling program was run by the Student Counseling Service, staffed by three professionally trained specialists. The goals of this service were to help a student

build more positive self-concepts and feelings about himself; become more proficient in decision making about his educational and career goals and modes of action to obtain these goals ... and [explore] possible needs for developmental experiences. . . . Emphasis is placed on all of the community and college resources so that opportunities are provided to students to satisfy their academic, career and psychosocial needs.

The above statement appeared in both the faculty and student handbooks and was read to students during the orientation meeting preceding the first week of classes. After the reading, the students were advised in a speech by the dean of students:

They [the counselors] are not shrinks. Please don't feel it's a stigma to go to them. [Laughter] They are here not only to deal with extraordinary problems which come up at one time or another, but they also deal with the normal problem of students. Your life at City Community College is going to be an adventure. It will be filled with surprises—pleasant ones and not so pleasant ones. And we're going to make mistakes, but let's try to learn from our mistakes as we try to make this school work.

Students reacted to the dean's short speech with either silence or brief, cynical laughter. Having just been told their self-concepts, decision-making abilities, and "developmental experiences" all left something to be desired and that because of this a great many resources would be mobilized to meet their "psycho-social needs," there was no polite applause (as there was for other school officials) when the three counselors were introduced on stage. If these three strangers were not "shrinks," they were close relatives.

The reaction of students to counseling, whether formal or informal, in or out of class, was resentment. They were, in a word, insulted. It is one thing to doubt one's intelligence or self-esteem, but it is quite another thing to imply that one's psyche is faulty. At no time during the year's fieldwork was a student observed equating lack of academic motivation or inability with psychological abnormality, and at no time during the year was counseling well received by the majority of the students. For example, half of the class did not do the five-page self-analysis assignment described earlier and of those who did, some manufactured false data, others purposefully kept their reports superficial, and two students analyzed a character from a novel. The following incident describes two students' responses to the assignment:

> Before class I am talkng with Bill in the hallway when Rick comes along. Bill says, "Hey, man, how do you feeeel!" We laugh and I ask Bill which option he chose for the assignment. He says it won't be about himself because "That's none of her fuckin' business." He adds that there is nothing "goofy" about himself and if there were he'd certainly not put it on paper.
>
> I say that assignment doesn't necessarily have to say something negative. Rick says, "But that's what she wants. She's always trying to get inside your head, like there's a screw loose."

As for the Self-Awareness Workshop, well advertised through a student newsletter, reminders given in class, and letters mailed home, not one student attended:

> I go to the second floor lounge where the business students are to meet but find only [business teachers, the chairman, the dean of students, and one of the full-time counselors]. _____ [the counselor] tells me that previously they met with 12 students: "It was a real good meeting. They've been having a lot of trouble with their teachers and courses and we discussed how they could do better, if they should be in some other program, things like that. We finally decided to set up this search group." He explains that students can participate in this counseling program for the next five weeks in lieu of some of their classes and that part of the program is to be a series of encounter groups. The meeting was called for 11:00; at 11:20 no students have yet appeared. There is some talk about how they do not understand why this has happened. The Dean suggests they go to the faculty lounge to talk. They leave without looking at me. I get the feeling I am not invited and that they are embarrassed.
>
> [The next day] I tell Mike and Steve that I went to the workshop meeting, but that no students came. They laugh. I ask why they didn't go. Mike says he wouldn't want to talk about himself in front of

everybody. I ask if he would prefer to do it on a one-to-one basis and he replies that he would only go to _____ [name of teacher] if he had a problem with course work. Steve agrees. Mike says, "I have my feet closer to the ground than that ding-a-ling _____ [name of one of the three counselors].

Counseling was not a strategy peculiar to City Community College, for like small four-year institutions, junior colleges in the United States traditionally have emphasized the need "to administer to the personal needs and problems of each student."[4] That this extends beyond academic and career advice is made clear by Leonard Koos in his national survey of community college "student personnel programs." His conclusion is worth presenting as it reveals the same "change the victim" ideology undergirding both the formal and classroom counseling efforts at CCC:

> A larger proportion of students in community than in four-year colleges have disabilities in skills in reading, language, mathematics, and study. Larger proportions come from families of lower social status and have a high incidence of economic problems and/or lower motivation for continued attendance. The need for guidance in respect to personal qualities and attitudes is less apparent because of the relative intangibility and the limited research concerning them, although these restrictions can hardly minimize their importance.[5]

Despite seeing the social class system as the prime source of students' values and behavior, the liberal teachers who used counseling clearly opted for the psychologistic response legitimized in the community college system. Although the manifest function of this ideology was to counter the alleged psychological defects produced by lower-class life the latent function was to align students' perceptions and values with those of their teachers:

> I try to make them think positive about things, to have good feelings. They tell me that they are feeling good about themselves and each other, but then I look at the atmosphere of the classroom and it's just dead. If only I could get through.
>
> (a social science teacher)

> An awful lot of what I do, even in the guise of an academic presentation of some intellectual idea is to try to develop self-awareness and a kind of confidence in living. I like to preach the idea that a person is capable of being happy and maintaining a high level of self-esteem in any rung of the social ladder; so I don't particularly appeal to students to get an upper-middle-class job. Obviously you can't do that

in the career programs, but I have a strong feeling that regardless of the initial objective of a career program or whatever occupation the student is purportedly being prepared for, I think it ought to be an open-ended thing, not a terminal education, but something that if they've responded and they have developed an intellectual curiosity they can use that as a basis for continuing their education, not as a dead-end street. For keeping their minds alive even if they don't go on to college, that's what I mean. That's why I do what I call academic social work. If I can get them to, you know, know thyself, then we can go to do what I want to do, the academic component.

(a social science teacher)

Once I realized I couldn't teach the course content on the level I wanted to, I talked with _____ and _____ [two counselors] and decided to approach the students psychologically. Instead of teaching literature as literature I *used* the literature to try to get the kids to see who they were and how they could bring out their own potential, so that I teach course material at the same time that I try to deal with the students psychologically.

(an English teacher)

The Radical Perspective

Four of the five teachers who taught from a radical perspective were under 30, the sixth was 32; three taught social science courses and three taught English. All had participated in or were sympathetic to the radical student politics of the late 1960s. Like the liberal teachers, they located the source of students' difficulties in the social system and had lowered course standards and inflated grades. Rather than taking a psychologistic approach, however, they attempted to sensitize students to the causes and consequences of various social and political problems, hoping that this new consciousness would emancipate students and produce new agents of social change:

One thing I feel very happy with here is the lower- and lower-middle-class student, the lower-class *white* student. He's really where the action is in terms of—what's a nice word—consciousness raising. I don't like to use "radicalizing" around here because it turns people off.... I think that being a very political person—personally very political—I see this kind of creativity and consciousness raising or in changing people as a very important element.... You see we've got that triple job. We've got to get them jobs and we also have to teach them, so we have that vocational element. [We have to be] guiding them towards the kinds of things to do to fit them into society. That's one of our roles. But on the other hand our second role is to teach them academically responsible stuff. But then the third is what I was trying to get at ... my own personal thing which is, you want to call it conversion, you want to call it changing minds, consciousness raising. In other words I've given up personally on the idea of ethical neutralism, you know, although my personality is so flexible that I can bend with people. There's no question that I would try to persuade, but I think everybody does it in their own way, they just don't admit it.... I'm very lucky that I'm teaching the courses that I am such as community problems where I can teach them something about Saul Alinsky. I've settled on conflict theory as the only theory that works. And therefore, I guide a lot of my material that way and if I'm teaching about community problems I'll teach them about power and I would use something like Alinsky as a model, as a way of community change. So in that sense you're really using a person with non-middle-class values as a model—although they may opt for the middle class. But even if they opt, you see, I think you've got a problem. I think most of the students really would like to be middle class, they would aspire to that. You can't trample on their aspiration level and that's fair enough, but, you see, what I would like to see is for them to be angry. If I could get them angry at the middle class and not ruin their aspiration level but also get them angry at a lot of things, that is, angry at consumer problems, angry at political problems, I think that's a maximum accomplishment. I think it would be disillusionary to think that you're really going to create a core of proletariat revolutionaries at the community college because I don't think a teacher has that much effect. I think something would have to happen to that person to make a person that angry. It would have to be a personal experience. But what I'm really saying is that I want them to know that sometimes conflict and disorder are a healthy thing. You shouldn't play it down. Now that of course is very un-middle class; the middle-class thing is to reduce conflict, to prevent disorder. So even though I'm preparing them for a middle-class job with an agency I hope I'm preparing them in such a way that they will not fall right into that job, that they will become an adversary, an angry person in that job who would take that agency and turn it around. In other words, like law is middle class—as a profession—and law protects the middle class, but a lawyer doing legal service or legal aid is really using the law in a very exciting way. It's that kind of approach that I would see my teaching role as doing.

(a social science teacher)

I think that what bothers me [about the students] is that they are so passive and don't take stands in their lives which I don't think is only a [social] class thing either. I think that's true of Americans or of people living in capitalist society. I want them to get to see, to consider the whole, that things don't just happen to be the way they are —there's some reason behind it, and to see where they can take action in their own lives. . . . [I don't] want to move them up a notch so that there's somebody else at the bottom. [I want] them to realize that the whole system—well, first of all I would like them to realize that if they made $25,000 a year instead of $14,000 a year it wouldn't lead to happiness. If I could just somehow—poof!—get that into people's heads, it would be a good start. You see what I'm doing is much more political in nature because I want them to know what's going on in terms of power so that in some kind of way they can make decisions really knowing what the real issues are.

(a social science teacher)

I think that teaching is an incredibly egotistical profession and I obviously turn on to students who somehow like my ideas or who come to me and say, "I've been changed by this or radicalized some way or could I have more reading from so and so" or things like that. . . . For example, literature just ends up being an extreme reflection of what the social and cultural values are. I think that what I attempt to do in my course is raise a political consciousness more than a psychological consciousness though obviously they're closely intertwined. What I'm much more concerned about is that people, *all of us,* start questioning where we find ourselves and for what reasons outside of our own control—like what class we are born into. . . . And you know what I think is important is one, that people see the value of where they come from and secondly, to understand exactly how powerful or powerless they are. I feel that in terms of politicizing people and making them aware of the system one of the most powerful places is in an educational setting like this, not in organizing as much, not helping welfare rights, maybe because that's been done and it's overloaded, but because it's at a point where people are over a barrel and you present an alternative, in that maybe they will grab on to it because that's all they have. Well here you just allow them a chance to at least start thinking about things.

(an English teacher)

Political consciousness raising in the classroom usually was attempted through analyses of such social problems as racism, poverty, social class injustice, and the camouflaging of "the real issues" by the U.S. political process. Rather than being strident or sloganeering, these teachers patiently tried to nourish a vision of a society in which people were no longer oppressed and exploited. However patient and noble, radical teachers eventually had to challenge students' political and ideological beliefs—and they met much resistance. In addition to the absences, low levels of effort, and incivility described earlier, these teachers often found themselves defending their views against a class of mostly conservative and hostile students. The following is an example of but one class:

Goldstein begins by asking about the reading. The first student he calls on says he has not done the reading. He calls on a second student who says, "Wait. Let me look at it," as he opens his book. He offers a short comment.

The topic for today is urban blight and how it spreads—what happens to a community as blight spreads and why landlords and tenants let property go. The students answer his questions, but they are hesitant. There are some long pauses. They have not yet specifically referred to the reading assignments. Goldstein is trying to make the point that ownership of property is the key. They are talking in very simplistic terms. They are talking in terms of the *virtues* of ownership.

Goldstein: "What about if a group owns the property—would they feel a sense of community and commitment? What do you think, Margaret?"

Margaret: "Ya, I think it could work." That is all she has to say.

Goldstein discusses blockbusing. Two students say that is happening in their neighborhoods now. Goldstein asks a number of questions; the students offer very short answers. If not "ya" or "no" then they offer a sentence or two; there is no interest on the students' part to push a conversation. They discuss why blacks are moving out of _____ [a section of the city] and this generates some conversation. Two students in the rear have their own conversation for the first half hour of the class. The class discussion turns to why blacks are not in certain occupations: fire, police, rapid transit, trade unions. It is the male students who do the talking; they say it is because blacks are lazy, they don't want to work. In an *attempt to reduce their prejudices* against blacks Goldstein tries to more rationally explain the phenomenon. He is not only explaining (in a very simplistic manner) the societal constraints confronted by blacks, but he is also emphasizing that the students' feelings towards blacks are ill-founded. This is very explicit. Of course, he fails to reduce their animosity—his arguments only make the students more vehement. The discussion turns briefly to women's liberation. One male student declares that he is not sexist, but then goes on to refer to women as *chicks*. There is no laughter as no one seems to notice this contradiction. Subgroups begin their own debates on the "black question." Goldstein's control over the class is lost.

[Later that day while discussing his class] Goldstein says, "I think I'm getting somewhere, even if just a little bit." He holds his fingers an inch apart—like calipers.

(a social science class)

Such confrontations allowed these teachers to see themselves as embattled missionaries: Having identities as both teachers and "radicals" they were able to infuse their work with a moral charge they believed would sustain them through their adversity.[6]

INEFFECTIVE RATIONALIZATIONS

In the earlier discussion of teachers' career paths, it was pointed out that learning institutional meanings and rhetoric is not the same as internalizing or having an unquestioned faith in them. Indeed, that the three perspectives described above were responses to occupational contingencies does not allow us to assume that they were *effective* responses, that is, that for individual teachers they resolved or minimized the problems that spawned them in the first place. For some teachers, perspectives in fact did not work well; hence, their "explanations and solutions" for the career switch, for students' behavior, and for their own approach to students did not adequately soften the blow of reality. In speaking of what they call "cool alternation," Peter Berger and Thomas Luckmann describe the consequences for an individual's identity of this predicament:

> It follows that one's own institutionalized conduct may be apprehended as "a role" from which one may detach oneself in one's own consciousness, and which one may "act out" with manipulative control . . . the situation, then, has a much more far reaching consequence than the possibility of individuals playing at being what they are *not* supposed to be. They also play at being what they *are* supposed to be —a quite different matter.[7]

Some teachers, then, became aware that they were using their explanations and solutions not only for students' "best interests" but for their own purposes as well. With this awareness, some teachers detached or disidentified themselves from their own roles and acknowledged the insincerity with which they were playing them; the existential character of this social dilemma is evident in the excerpts from the recorded interviews below.

Most of the excerpts are responses to the last question on the interview schedule, "Do you ever have to rationalize to yourself why you are teaching here? By rationalize, I mean do you ever have to offer yourself reasons or justifications for teaching here which you do not sincerely believe or accept?" Seven teachers answered affirmatively, and with little if any further prodding discussed at length this sensitive issue; whether there were others unwilling or unable to reveal themselves in this way makes it impossible to know the extent to which the affirmative replies are representative. As Hughes has stated:

> The language about work is . . . loaded with value and prestige judgments and with defensive choice of symbols . . . the value-weighting

in popular speech is natural and proper, for concealment and ego protection are of the essence of social intercourse.... And part of the problem of method in the study of work behavior is that the people who have the most knowledge about a given occupation ... and from whom therefore the data for analysis must come, are the people in the occupation. They may combine in themselves a very sophisticated manipulative knowledge of the appropriate social relations, with a very strongly motivated suppression, and even repression, of the deeper truths about their relationships, and, in occupations of higher status, with great verbal skill in keeping these relationships from coming up for thought and discussion by other people.[8]

These excerpts are exceptional because, if even briefly, defenses were dropped; changes in voice, eye contact, and posture subjectively indicated teachers' awareness of the heresies they were expressing and that earlier statements were being contradicted. It was is if they were saying, "OK, I gave you the official line before, but this is how I really feel."

The Conservative Teachers

As noted, the four conservative teachers believed that because there was little to be done for unmotivated or untalented students, they should concentrate on their best students without lowering standards or inflating grades. One of these four was willing to admit that this strategy returned too few dividends:

Well, for me [pause] ya, that's a pretty sensitive question because I've been doing that kind of rationalizing a good deal of my life. I've always seen myself as being somewhat misplaced, perhaps under-placed. I have reasons for feeling misplaced. One of them is not having finished my doctorate, that's purely personal, but perhaps there's some relationship between that and being here. But, [long pause] I suppose that in an ideal situation I would prefer being in an environment where it was more exciting intellectually.... I don't get the feeling I must reach toward them [the students] and I must extend myself and you know, stretch myself. I don't get that feeling ... I enjoy the good students, but I can't tell you I get great satisfaction from them either. There aren't very many.
  Interviewer: Satisfactions?
  Teacher: Good students. Really good.
  Interviewer: And that makes you feel—
  Teacher: To that extent, yes, everyday when I come in here I have to close my eyes a little bit.

(an English teacher)

The Liberal Teachers

Five liberal teachers admitted doubting their own liberal justifications for teaching in the community college. In one instance a teacher who had withdrawn from a doctoral program claimed that after taking his first community college job he decided to concentrate on discovering the best way to teach his academic subject area to poorer students rather than on continuing research in the substantive area itself:

> The only soul-searching part, and I guess it's a question that will never be answered since I have no intention of ever getting a Ph.D., or at least if I ever do get a Ph.D. certainly not in pure _____ [academic area], the thing I'll never know is whether deep down inside it was a cop-out; in other words maybe it was I have no faith in myself as a _____ researcher and felt that this would be a nice way to hide.... I have done [many things] in the field of _____ where I really brought education to the community ... but I mean it was my way of saying to myself that maybe I really—that it wasn't a cop-out.... I was never sure whether it was to escape the pressure of living up to a _____ [university] research image.... I think that what really happened in my life was that professionally I was two people: I was _____ [name] the researcher and _____ the educator.... The only regret that I've had, and I think this is a human kind of thing, I think of the quotation that, "a man's reach must exceed his grasp or what is heaven for?" ... I have dreamt of making education my life's work [originally, it was research] and I felt it would take me a lifetime to get there, but through good fortune in many ways I sort of reached fairly great heights at a relatively young age. For example, I came to _____ [another community college] as an instructor with just a Bachelor's degree and in just six years I was already a full professor having been promoted every two years from the time that I got there. I turned down higher promotions because by my way of life any higher promotion was no longer a promotion—it took me out of my field. I was full professor and chairman of the department of _____ [and that] is by my standards the highest I could go. Being a dean already takes me into a new field, you see. And then what happened was that the regret that came in was that once you've reached these heights it doesn't seem it was that hard to get there. In other words, you look ahead and you say, "Boy, it would really be something to accomplish all of this." Then suddenly when you've accomplished it you look back and the years telescope; and I had a period of uneasiness that almost gave me ... almost disturbed me mentally. I mean it was not quite that serious, but almost, *where I really believed I could have been both.* In other words, once I reached

the peaks I had as an educator, my feeling was, you know I could have done this and still been a good research _____ [subject area].*

Other teachers did not specifically mention the loss of the research role, but instead questioned the school's ability to effectively intervene in the lives of students (which, of course, is at the heart of their liberal ideology), and consequently found it difficult to infuse their work with meaning. Among these teachers were those who earlier had placed so much hope in the idea that students would at least get "something" from their courses:

Let me say it's taken a sense of adjustment. I've never had any direct relationship with a community college before. I find that there are things about a community college that are different. That is, one perceives even with the community college itself that there's not as much of a premium placed on [pause] on developing a student's intellectual capacity; that is, of straining a student's intellectual capacity so that he *really does grow,* not just that he fills in the gaps or voids that are already there. That takes a bit of adjustment, sure. Do I rationalize about it? Ya, I think so. There are times when I've been very unhappy about it. I can't talk about this with my colleagues because I think they're more committed to the community college than I can be. I have spoken about this to _____ [the president of City Community College] because I have had thoughts about leaving. I think that the kind of quick uptake that you get with an idea at a school with more mature students around and with a more settled faculty is something I miss.

(a history teacher)

It's pretty hard to rationalize, I mean I do what I do because I enjoy it. I studied _____ [academic area] because I enjoy it. It's a very selfish reason perhaps, but everything is that way. But it's not enough just for me to say, "I'm here because I like it." It's necessary at some point to say, "What I'm doing is valid, I can help people in some way." That fact that it is not necessary even to get into a four-year college or it's not going to be practical in their day-to-day lives. . . . I think it's only normal that I would become somewhat paranoid and feel that I am being attacked. And how do you justify what you do? I mean finally in all honesty you say, "I do what I do because I like to do it." And if I can reach some student who has the same kind of makeup and who is going to find some kind of value in what I teach, then

---

*The career information in this passage does not allow the teacher to be identified by academic area.

that's valid. . . . But there aren't many of those around. . . . I'm sure they [teachers] find it very, very hard to say, "My God, I've invested this amount of money, this amount of hard work and time into this field that I like, which I do because I like it," and then they have poor students in front of them. And they say, "Well, what's it all worth? Where are we going?" I mean, the teachers who I've talked to who have been honest with me, stated quite categorically that they don't know how long they're going to remain here. . . . In other words, we can teach first- and second-year courses, but we can't teach a third-year course because they can get that in a four-year institution. That means you're limited and no one who has gone for a master's or a Ph.D. who has a particular area of interest, wants to spend the rest of their lives teaching basic writing or basic French grammar or survey courses in history or whatever. So if the possibility opened for these people to teach at an institution where they could teach some of these courses that interest them more, I don't care if they admit it or not, I'm sure they'd take it. As far as the students, I don't think we could take it forever.

(a humanities teacher)

I think if I said it was a dumb question I would be kidding myself. Yes, I do have to rationalize. I really do. I think that if I didn't rationalize I would probably go stark, raving loony at times. I have found myself doing it more and more frequently since September. In September I rationalized I needed the job: I was married, owned a home. . . . Many days I say to myself, "Why am I going there? Why?" And the only thing that saves me are my better students. . . . I know that if I couldn't relate to the better students I would quit. I would have resigned, because I would not have been helping even them. I think I would have. I would have resigned because there would have been no sense of my being here at all.

(a social science teacher)

Well, I sometimes say to myself that the job that has to be done here is probably a greater job than has to be done in other colleges. I don't know if I really believe that or not. I say it sometimes to myself. I'm not quite convinced of it though. I'm not quite convinced of the community college as a concept. . . . [The students here] are the people who are going to be working for Blue Cross-Blue Shield, making $130 a week, and they'll be file clerks or something like that. So my point is that I think many of them could be doing much better if they were in trade school or if they were actually learning some sort of task, be it automotive repair or something like that. I think they'd be much better off. But I think something else too. I think that one thing the community college does is give you an opportunity you ordinarily wouldn't have or couldn't afford to have. So as a growth experience,

in terms of personal growth ... in terms of occupational direction ...
although I'm not quite sure of that either. That's one of my rational-
izations.

(a history teacher)

The Radical Teachers

One of the radical teachers questioned both the morality of attempting to convert working-class students and the possibility of effect-
ing social change. As with the conservative and liberal teachers, the
instructor traced her dilemma to an unreceptive audience:

In fact what I'm doing could be more harmful than anything else. I
made certain political assumptions about what would be the best
living situation for all of us in terms of society changing, and those
assumptions are very *alien* to my students. When you've been to the
class and had a lot of material rejected by them and say, "Look, they
didn't bring me happiness—." The whole thing about the Weather-
men in SDS—the big in-joke was that all their fathers made over
$100,000 a year. And you know, it's easy for me to say I've had that
experience, and that's not where it's at, and this is where I see the
changes to be made. I'm sitting with these students who are sweating
eight hours a day and have a real belief that these two years here are
going to make a radical, economic, control change. What are the
options for them? That's what I find most frightening. What am I
supposed to say to them? "You are going to have a low management
job. You're not going to go anywhere. You're going to be frozen there.
All you are going to do is feel guilt because you didn't succeed in
America...." I'm changing now. I think that was a mistake I made.
I think it's a mistake to make your classroom very political if you're
the one who is making it political, because that's the surest way to
shut people off. If they let someone like me, for example, know how
deep their sexism goes or their racism goes, that I am going to turn
around and fight them.
    Interviewer: There's sort of a resentment that builds up?
    Teacher: Yeah. And I think it's a justifiable resentment on their
part.

(a social science teacher)

The resentment this teacher sees and fears is of radical condenscen-
sion. If, on the one hand, she attempts to make students aware of their
sexism and racism, she risks being seen as a person who too self-
righteously believes in the superiority of her politics and morals; if, on
the other hand, she attempts to show students how they are victimized
by a class-based tracking system that denies them genuine opportunity

for upward mobility, she fears they will reject her for the guilt they will feel for not succeeding in America. Interestingly, although she might tell students it is the *class system* that denies them, she thinks they will still blame *themselves,* and furthermore, that they will resent her for bringing up the issue in the first place. This teacher, more than any other, came closest to understanding the students' dilemma as described in Chapter 1. When asked, after her last comment above, "How much does this bind bother you?" she replied:

> I can't tell you how much. When I think I'm not accomplishing what I want to accomplish or if I think that I'm banging my head against a stone wall or if I think I'm sick of not getting any gratification from this.

In this chapter so far we have investigated the mechanisms teachers used to sustain themselves in the face of what almost all agreed was an unanticipated and sorrowfully low level of student performance. For most teachers commitment to an ideologically premised perspective apparently shielded them from having their occupational identities upset. As but one further indication of this, none of these teachers planned to leave CCC in the foreseeable future. For the seven liberal arts and human services teachers who expressed ideological misgivings, however, the situation passed the point where the fracture between expectations and reality could be mended in the current setting. Having become conscious that their roles were cloaked with justifications they could not truly accept, and that the futility and artificiality they felt could not be resolved, all but one were privately preparing to resign from CCC within the next two years.*

THE VOCATIONAL TEACHERS

The vocational teachers were not as distressed by the students as were the liberal arts and human services teachers. The vocational instructors' previous occupational identities partly immunized them from the chagrin of their co-workers by allowing them to view students from two different roles, that of teacher and that of "practitioner." As teachers, they had difficulty coping with the problems posed by

---

*One was planning to return to graduate school, four mentioned four-year colleges and suburban two-year schools, and one was thinking of "elite" preparatory schools. No teachers cited administrative restrictions or personalities as a contributing factor in their wanting to leave CCC.

students, and in the interviews they expressed their frustration and occasionally their anger. As former "practitioners," however, they empathized with their charges and, unlike the liberal arts teachers, offered unsolicited praise for them; significantly, this praise was not for their qualities as students, but for their virtues as working-class people. To explore this phenomenon, it is first necessary to examine the socioeconomic background of the teachers.

On the basis of descriptions of their parents' occupations and education (as well as other information some spontaneously offered), teachers were designated as upper class, upper middle class, lower middle class, working class, and lower class.[9] As Table 5.1 indicates, 7 of the 9 vocational teachers were from the bottom two classes, whereas 26 of the 28 liberal arts and human services teachers were fairly evenly distributed among the three middle classes. As described in Chapters 3 and 4, the middle-class orientation of this latter group contributed to the tensions between them and their presumably mobile students. The vocational teachers, however, having backgrounds similar to their students' and preparing them for working-class occupations, could view them not only as students but as fellow travelers. (Exceptions are discussed below.)

That there was a common bond was evident in the shifting appraisals of students. At some points in the interviews, vocational teachers judged students as negatively as did the liberal arts teachers, yet oftentimes their perceptions abruptly switched and, seen from a different angle, students were lauded as "clean," "good kids," "fun-loving," or "industrious." (The teachers, of course, did not state that these characteristics were peculiar to working-class people; the datum lies in the teachers' praising students in the context of discussing their social class status.) The following are examples of this alternating criticism and praise:

> Interviewer: Were there any major discrepancies between your expectations of the academic caliber of students and what you actually found here?
> Teacher: I got the impression from some people, not the administration, that we were going to have a problem with the background of the students from _____ High and from _____ High [two inner-city schools] and from some of the other _____ [inner-city] schools, but I found, at least the first semester and right up to now, that some of the best students are from [those schools] and I think we were led astray in some things, that they were really the drudge of society, which they are not. Some of the cleanest kids I've ever seen are from _____ [inner-city area].

TABLE 5.1   Social Class Background of City Community College Teachers, by Curriculum Area

	Liberal Arts and Human Services Teachers	Vocational Teachers
Upper class	2	0
Upper middle class	7	0
Lower middle class	11	2
Working class	8	4
Lower class	0	3
Total	28	9

Source: U.S. Bureau of the Census, 1970.

Interviewer: Did you have to tone down your courses at all?

Teacher: Oh, ya. I think if you talk to Professor _____, I think he altered the complete math course, because they were terrible in some things.

Interviewer: Did you have to—?

Teacher: Some of them were so bad, they were just wasting their time....

Interviewer: Do they work as hard as you expected?

Teacher: I'm heavy on case studies and those kinds of things and they don't like to use the library, so consequently.... I was flattered the other day, the librarian said that my program uses the library more than any of the other occupational programs. I forced them into that, which they rebel against all the time. But they can be very industrious. I'm just slowly getting acclimated to the cheating and plagiarism and the conniving.

(a fire science teacher)

Teacher: The students here are not as, how should I say it—they're not as educationally good as I thought. I have to explain things very carefully and, you know, lower my standards such that they can do the work. It was very difficult the first three weeks figuring the level they were on. I really had to scale down my standards a lot.

Interviewer: Do students make it difficult and frustrating for you or do they make it relatively easy and comfortable for you to do what you would like to do?

Teacher: Oh, they're a good bunch of kids. They horse around too much, but that's the spunk from _____ [inner-city area]. They aren't what you'd call your good student, but they're alright. Good kids, they are.

(a law enforcement teacher)

Teacher: Sometimes in class they can really get on my nerves, like when they get silly and giggle. They complain endlessly. Sometimes a whole class just won't cooperate. But there's a sweetness about them too.
Interviewer: I thought you said they made it uncomfortable?
Teacher: They're just letting it out, having fun. It was the same at _____ [another city school where she taught part time].

(a secretarial teacher)

The business teachers did not have a working-class occupational role, but one of the four interviewed, because of his background, had similar alternating perceptions. As a recent graduate from a nearby university whose students are predominantly working and lower middle class, he stressed in the interview that he enjoyed teaching at City Community College because of his own working-class background. Furthermore, he shared his chairman's liberal perspective and stated forcefully that "any student, if you know how to talk to him, can be saved and trained for a better job than if he didn't come here." Claiming this special affinity, he attributed students' behavior and academic performance to the rambunctiousness, anti-intellectualism, and aggressiveness he thought characterized working-class males in particular. Because he defined these qualities as understandable and sometimes admirable, his professional identity was not in jeopardy, despite his complaints of how difficult students made his job.

A second business teacher, who had been recently admitted to the state bar, was so disturbed by the reduced opportunity to use his legal training and by his students' performance that he announced midway through the interview (before he could be asked) that he would be leaving at the end of the school year. Having a career before him as a lawyer he found it impossible to commit himself to community college teaching:

There's just a lot of absenteeism, a lack of preparation and in some cases it just seems like a total lack of concern with how they do in school. And it's more than a little bit, a little bit frustrating for a teacher.... [Later] Well, like I said, getting out of law school I was considering a number of other options and probably would have chosen another one if it was available. In that sense I have to say,

"You're here because [laughs] because it was the only acceptable alternative at the time."

(a business teacher)

Finally, the stockbroker who had come to the business department because of the market recession and his indignation at the brokerage industry admitted to considerable confusion and consternation about what he found at CCC. Throughout the interview he claimed his lack of preparation and expertise as a teacher made it impossible for him to explain the student behavior, which, he said, distressed him very much. At the same time, however, he claimed that being out of the brokerage business was so relieving that these problems were a welcome challenge:

> I have never once had a negative feeling about it [teaching] in the sense of saying, "Christ, I've made a mistake," or "This is more bother than it's worth." Certainly I've gotten in conditions where I've been jammed up . . . had a high anxiety level, but never one of regret. . . . But it is satisfying against a commission business background where even if you're working hard you can wind up making no money and have the boss on your back during bad times. So I've found it very interesting.

(a business teacher)

The perspectives of the four business teachers (including the chairman) varied with their background, career paths, and career stages. Although they subscribed to the liberal perspective of their chairman and did lower standards, inflate grades, and attempt counseling, they did not have the academic images the liberal arts teachers had to defend. For this same reason, with the exception of the lawyer who left because of his investment in another profession, all the vocational teachers, regardless of department, were subjectively less dismayed than their liberal arts co-workers.

NOTES

1. Everett C. Hughes, "Non-Economic Aspects of Academic Morale," in *Higher Education in the United States,* ed. Seymour E. Harris (Cambridge: Harvard University Press, 1960), pp. 118–20.

2. For a theoretical analysis of the relationship between occupations and ideologies, see Vernon K. Dibble, "Occupations and Ideologies," *American Journal of Sociology* 68 (September 1962): 229–41.

3. Christopher Jencks and David Riesman, *The Academic Revolution* (Garden City, N.Y.: Doubleday, 1969), p. 488.

4. Charles R. Monroe, *Profile of the Community College* (San Francisco: Jossey-Bass, 1972), p. 144.

5. Leonard V. Koos, *The Community College Student* (Gainesville, Fla.: University of Florida Press, 1970), p. 509.

6. For an impressionistic analysis of a similar perspective at a working-class four-year college, see John McDermott, "The Laying On of Culture," *Nation,* March 10, 1969, pp. 296–301. McDermott claims that unless teachers are keenly aware of the specific culture history and experiences of their students, attempts to make students more politically self-conscious will be resented and ignored.

7. Peter L. Berger and Thomas Luckmann, *The Social Construction of Reality: A Treatise in the Sociology of Knowledge* (Garden City, N.Y.: Doubleday, 1967), p. 173. (Emphasis in the original.)

8. Everett C. Hughes, "Work and Self," in *The Sociological Eye: Selected Papers* (Chicago: Aldine/Atherton, 1971), p. 339.

9. The system of occupational classification is based on Albert J. Reiss, *Occupations and Social Status* (New York: Free Press, 1961), pp. 54–57. The 90 rated occupations were divided into five groups. Additional family data given in the interviews (parents' education, family values) were correlated with the fivefold typology in Joseph Kahl, *The American Class Structure* (New York: Holt, Rinehart and Winston, 1965), pp. 187–217.

6
CONCLUSION:
THE "COOLING-OUT"
FUNCTION RECONSIDERED

If an advantage of exploratory fieldwork is maximizing the possibility of discovering and investigating the unexpected, then the chief surprise of this study was the importance for students and teachers of finding an acceptable social niche. Looking beneath the surface activity of education there appeared groups of people shedding, forfeiting, searching for, and settling into life courses, positions, and, in a fundamental sense, identities.[1] William Graham Sumner's classic definition of institutions as "functionaries set to cooperate in prescribed ways at a certain conjuncture" may apply to administrative acts and even to the meeting of the participants' informal expectations, but expectations are not always met or known in advance.[2] City Community College is better seen as a confluence or intertwining of social dramas. Indeed, this investigation has focused on the determinants, content and intensity of various hopes as well as disappointments; and of how they were woven into the fabric of the school's culture.

Viewing the community college this way calls for a reconsideration of Burton Clark's classic essay on the public junior college.[3] According to Clark, democratic societies ask individuals "to act as if social mobility were universally possible," the belief being that social status and other rewards accrue to those who try.[4] Then, borrowing from Robert Merton, Clark argues that democratic societies also limit and block culturally instilled goals, and that mechanisms are needed to deflect the resentment and mollify the disappointment of those to whom opportunity is denied to induce them to take less rewarding work. For Clark, a major function of two-year colleges is to cool students' aspirations and temper their frustrations through the gradually accumulated evidence (achievement tests, vocational aptitude tests, course grades, teachers' recommendations, counselors' advice) that they ought to change to a terminal vocational curriculum rather than transfer to a four-year institution.

Clark's analysis is based on his larger study of San Jose Junior College.[5] His sources of data included "informal discussions ... with administrative personnel of the headquarters of the San Jose Unified School District, with administrators of the San Jose Junior College, and with approximately one-fourth of the college's teaching staff."[6] Although human respondents were helpful, "records and memoranda became in this study the primary source of dependable material."[7] The documents relied on were school board minutes, "a perusal of available policy memoranda, a study of state reports and newspaper accounts."[8] Finally, a questionnaire was mailed to the faculty (the return rate is not given), "but it was, in fact, a late appendage to the study, and the basic interpretation of the character of the college was derived before the survey results were available."[9] In his article (drawn from his book) the only sources of data are quotations from administrative reports and handbooks. Clark gives no indication of having observed a class or of having talked to a single student. Consequently, his analysis of the "cooling-out" function is, in a word, distorted.

The series of counseling sessions he outlines may well be accurate, assuming that the teacher-counselors of San Jose Junior College did not meet the resistance given those at City Community College. So, too, there is no reason to question the percentage of students who Clark reports as having changed from a transfer to a vocational curriculum. The distortions are that the "cooling-out" function actually does resolve disappointment and resentment and that students who remain in the transfer (liberal arts) program are untroubled by the prospect of social mobility. As described in Chapter 3, the training students who were "cooled-out" in high school, or even earlier, were clearly conscious of and wounded by past failures and their low self regard. As discussed in Chapter 4, the majority of males in the Liberal Arts program were quite anxious over the consequences of both failure and success.

Because the students of San Jose Junior College were of approximately the same social background (74 percent were from lower-white-collar, upper-blue-collar, and lower-blue-collar families), it is difficult to accept the assertions that the "cooling-out" function works as smoothly as Clark insists.[10] Says Clark:

> The students themselves help to keep this function concealed by wishful unawareness. Those who cannot enter other colleges but still hope to complete four years will be motivated at first not to admit the cooling out process to consciousness. Once exposed to it, they again will be led not to acknowledge it, and so they are saved insult to their self-image.

In summary, the cooling-out process in higher education is one whereby systematic discrepancy between aspiration and avenue is covered over and stress for the individual is minimized. The provision of readily available alternative achievements in itself is an important device for alleviating the stress consequent on failure and so preventing anomic and deviant behavior.[11]

Contrary to Clark, the data in this study indicate that the "cooling-out" function does not work well and that the concerns of social class and personal responsibility militate against wishful unawareness. Certainly the students described here would like to escape insult and pain, but what they said in effect was that such an escape was dreadfully difficult and that the wounds of blocked opportunity fester rather than heal. To say that students repress such unpleasant thoughts is perhaps a bit of wishful unawareness by those who would subscribe to the harmlessness of the "cooling-out" function.[12] To the contrary, stress and anomie and deviant behavior were evident in the students' resistance to their schoolwork, in their absenteeism, in their "assaults" on teachers, and in their self-criticisms. This is not to say that students were always explicitly self-conscious of the "cooling-out" process or that they could locate and articulate the social sources of their tensions. As Max Weber, in his classic "Definition of Sociology and Social Action," states:

In the great majority of cases actual action goes on in a state of inarticulate half-consciousness or actual unconsciousness of its subjective meaning. The actor is more likely to "be aware" of it in a vague sense than he is to "know" what he is doing or be explicitly self-conscious about it. . . . Only occasionally and, in the uniform action of large numbers, often only in the case of a few individuals, is the subjective meaning of the action, whether rational or irrational, brought clearly into consciousness. . . . But the difficulty need not prevent the sociologist from systematizing his concepts by the classification of possible types of subjective meaning. That is, he may reason as if action proceeded on the basis of clearly self-conscious meaning.[13]

The dramas of students and teachers (at least the liberal arts and human services teachers) intertwine because the latter have also been cooled-out, but, again, not with complete success. By making the necessary changes, Clark's description of how students are sidetracked and offered an alternative career track applies equally well to those teachers who apparently had made a successful career change:

> Here the cooling-out process is built into the system. Its effect is to let down hopes gently and unexplosively. Through it [teachers] find their occupational and academic futures being redefined.... The drawn-out denial, when it is effective is in place of a personal, hard ("No"); instead the [teacher] is brought to realize, finally, that it is best to ease himself out of the competition.... [14]

An ineffective denial, at least for the teachers of CCC, brought on an existential problem similar to that of their students. Confronted by an alternative that in the face of some larger reference group continuously ratified their private doubts, neither group could be secure with themselves or with each other. This perhaps allows us to see in all its intricacies what Willard Waller meant in his oft-quoted observation that the fundamental problem of schools is the "struggle of students and teachers to establish their own definitions of situations in the life of school."[15] That this struggle has no end and that situational definitions need not be once and for all acceptable to those who put them forth was also recognized by Waller when, in an earlier passage, he declared:

> The whole social order may be seen as a tangle of interlocking selves. Every man must have some pride, and he must have some relationship in which he really lives. Defeated on one surface of the tetrahedron, he grows into another. When a thousand men come together, each striving to establish an equilibrium of superiority and inferiority in a multitude of activities, each continually altering his participation in those activities and revising from moment to moment the psychic weighting of that participation, each striving to obtain for himself a favorable balance of trade in that coin with which social debts are mostly paid, namely, praise, and each disturbing the equilibrium which every other has worked out, when a thousand men live together, then each man lives a thousand lives.[16]

NOTES

1. The importance of looking beneath the official functions of an institution has been well stated by Everett Hughes: "Organization is always a combination of concealing and revealing, not all of it fully or consciously intended. When purposes are so strongly stated and seemingly so agreed upon as those of educational enterprises, we social scientists have learned to be particularly wary. We modify our methods in such a way as to be fooled as little as possible by that part of people's sentiments and doings which appears above the surface. I have long made it a rule not to commence the study of any collective enterprise or institution by careful perusal of all the rule books, constitutions, charters and by-laws, but rather by looking at some of the stresses and strains in the ongoing life of the enterprise." *Students' Culture and Perspectives: Lectures on Medical and General Education* (Lawrence, Kans.: University of Kansas Press, 1961), pp. 1–2.

2. William Graham Sumner, *Folkways* (Boston: Ginn, 1906), p. 53.

3. Burton Clark, "The 'Cooling-Out' Function in Higher Education," *American Journal of Sociology* 65 (May 1960): 569–76.

4. Ibid., p. 569.

5. Burton Clark, *The Open Door College: A Case Study* (New York: McGraw-Hill, 1960).

6. Ibid., p. 180.

7. Ibid., p. 181.

8. Ibid.

9. Ibid.

10. Ibid., pp. 54–55.

11. Clark, "The 'Cooling-Out' Function," p. 576.

12. Also, in fairness to Clark, he does not say he approves of the "cooling-out" function in a sociopolitical sense; it is that he does not acknowledge the difficulties students have in allowing themselves to be cooled-out. Recent studies of blue-collar workers suggest that even adults of this socioeconomic status have not been successfully cooled-out; that is, that they do not accept their lot with equanimity. For example, see Richard Sennett and Jonathan Cobb, *The Hidden Injuries of Class* (New York: Random House, 1972); Stanley Aronowitz, *False Promises: The Shaping of Working-Class Consciousness* (New York: McGraw-Hill, 1973); and Peter Binzen, *Whitetown, U.S.A.* (New York: Random House, 1970).

13. Guenther Ross and Claus Wittrich, eds., *Max Weber: Economy and Society* (New York: Bedminster Press, 1968), vol. 2, pp. 932–33.

14. Clark, "The 'Cooling-Out' Function in Higher Education," p. 574.

15. Willard Waller, *The Sociology of Teaching* (New York: Wiley, 1932), p. 297.

16. Ibid., p. 194.

APPENDIX A
METHODOLOGICAL PROBLEMS
AND PROCEDURES

I have decided to include this somewhat lengthy methodological appendix because too often in reports of field research readers are left with no clear idea of how data were actually gathered or of what practical problems and frustrations were encountered by the investigator. Such considerations are important not only for assessing the validity of data and interpretations but for what they may teach others about doing field work. While it may appear odd to report such things as that the men's room was occasionally the best sanctuary for writing field notes, or that attempts to fund the study had to be abandoned, my hope is that the sharing of the inglorious and the mundane, along with the satisfactions and joys, will illustrate how human the process of field research is.

In the spring of 1973 I audited a course on the governance of community colleges taught by the recently appointed president of City Community College. Several times during the semester he stressed the importance of administrators' "feeling the pulse" of the school, which, he said, could be facilitated by an open, nonauthoritarian bureaucratic structure and by better institutional research. After one class in which he discussed these things at length, I informed him of my interest in doing my doctoral research on the culture of CCC. Although I wanted to arrange a meeting to discuss the project, he suggested I send him a prospectus and a resume. Believing it important to assuage any fears he might have and to state clearly the conditions under which the research would be conducted, the following was included as part of a cover letter:

> Let me say a little about the study and how I envision my hoped for relation with City Community College. To conduct our study I will, in effect, need a license from City Community College to be anywhere and everywhere. I will want to informally associate with students, faculty and administrators in and out of class rooms, offices, hallways and lunch rooms. I will want to sit in on various student, faculty and administrative meetings. At times I will request more formal interviews. Obviously (and ethically) I will be constrained by certain obligations. All individuals (as well as the name and location of the school) will remain anonymous. In keeping with the scientific ethic the final report will be available to all who care to read it, but only with the greatest care not to injure or jeopardize anyone. Furthermore, I will in no significant way disrupt the day to day operation of the school. I have no desire to become a nuisance; I wish to observe

people under no more stress than they already experience. As I cannot be everywhere at once, there will be but a relatively few minutes each week for people to be free of me. I make no financial or space requests of the school. Finally, I think it desirable to fully reveal my role as researcher to those who become the objects of my attention. To be above suspicion is to be able to ask and learn what others may not.

The project can be viewed as a bargain. I ask to be tolerated on certain terms so that I may be free to observe and analyze. If I were asked to simplify and assess the ultimate meaning of this study I think I would say that those who read the report (including yourself and your colleagues who are the other parties to the bargain) will have the opportunity to view the college from different perspectives —those of the students, faculty, administrators and sociologist. Through each set of eyes the college will appear somehow different. In drawing a new line through social facts one reveals a new layer or peculiar dimension of social reality. In saying, "Yes, that's how it is, but I've never seen it that way before," we all can better manage our affairs and the affairs of our society.

In retrospect, the tone of the letter was somewhat obsequious; however, two weeks later the president told me I was welcome to do my research at CCC.

FUNDING

Unsuccessful attempts were made to secure funds from the National Institute of Education, the National Science Foundation, the State Board of Community Colleges, and a number of private foundations. Only the private agencies cited reasons for their rejections, usually stating that the project was not practically oriented (that is, not sufficiently geared to instituting new programs) and that they did not fund "pure" research. Once CCC opened, the time-consuming search for aid had to be abandoned and the fieldwork begun. Without funds to hire interviewers and secretarial help, the project was not as comprehensive as originally planned. Among the sacrifices were studies of the school's administrators, contacts with other nonacademic institutions, and the dropout problem; countless hours were instead spent typing field notes and transcribing recorded interviews.

ENTRANCE TO THE FIELD

Five weeks before school began, an appointment was made with the dean of students to discuss the study and what she knew of the student body. Equally important, I wanted to meet her and the other administrators to be certain they knew of the study and to secure from them their cooperation. She told me that the president had indeed informed the deans and other administrators of the study and that he requested they help in this project. Later I was introduced to several administrators as "the young man who is going to study our school." Learning there would be no advance faculty meeting in which I could be introduced (some teachers arrived in the city very late), the assistant dean of faculty suggested he write an article about the project in the weekly "Faculty Newsletter." The article appeared as follows:

> Howard London, a doctoral student, is currently conducting his dissertation using City Community College as a case study. His research here will continue throughout the year and will involve talking with students and staff, sitting in on classes, and conducting interviews with faculty. Basically, he is studying the development of a student culture here hoping to ascertain how a community college is experienced by students. Howard has an impressive background in sociology and is quite familiar with sociological research techniques including participant observation. He would appreciate any assistance you can render to him and has promised to share his findings with the college community.

My first contact with students was one week before classes, during the registration and orientation program. Since workmen were putting the finishing touches on the City Community College building, the program was held in a YMCA three blocks from the school. After a few moments' casual conversation with students, I would identify myself by name and ask in which subject the student was majoring. In return, I was almost always asked the same or similar questions, which would allow me to state that I was not a City Community College student, but a graduate student studying the first year of the school's operation. If asked for more information I would say I was studying what happens in the school on a day-to-day basis and what students think of the school. Throughout the year I would meet students in this manner in the hallways, in the cafeteria, in the lounge, and even in the men's room. As I became known by more students, it was not uncommon for students to introduce me to their friends (discussed below).

My standard introduction to teachers was similar, although after the newsletter was distributed I would often say, "I'm the one from Boston College who is studying City Community—the guy described in the Newsletter." If they did not remember the article or had not read the newsletter, I described the study as a year-long investigation of the culture of CCC. During these encounters I asked teachers' permission to visit their classes, explaining that I would always ask again on the days I wanted to come. There were no refusals.

Students initially seemed more suspicious of me than their teachers. They asked more questions about the study, wanting to know if I was part of the school administration, who was paying me, and if I reported to the dean. All my explanations were designed to convince students I was not someone who would compromise or injure them and that the chief reason for my spending an entire academic year in the school was to understand the school from their point of view.

One of my favorite explanations was to ask if they had ever answered a questionnaire in which none of the choices to the questions seemed to fit. Never receiving a negative reply, I would then explain that the people who wrote the questions probably spent little or no time with the people they were questioning, and so were unaware of the mistakes they had made. Yet they then would run all the answers through a computer and come up with what they thought was "the truth." I explained that the best way I could avoid that kind of mistake was to spend a great deal of time at CCC getting to know people. It is difficult to gauge the reaction of this explanation except to say that most students cited examples of the kinds of questionnaires I had described and others offered brief remarks, such as "That's really cool that you're doing that." Undoubtedly there were some who at some point or perhaps for the entire year thought I was a snooper who could not be trusted.

ROLES AND ETHICAL PROBLEMS

I played six roles during the year: complete participant, participant as observer, observer as participant, complete observer, adviser, and informant.[1] During the course of a typical day I often played all or most of these roles and even during the course of a single conversation would move from one role to another.

Complete Participant

Although it was my policy to inform everyone of my identity as a researcher soon after I met them, I sometimes could not explain myself soon enough and was mistaken for a fellow student. For example, students sometimes began conversations by complaining about a teacher or another student before I had an opportunity to introduce myself. On other occasions I was talking with someone who knew my identity when a friend who did not would join the conversation. Only three or four times did I purposefully delay revealing myself (and then only for a few minutes) in order to conduct a covert interview.

Ethically and methodologically I wanted to avoid having students who had shared confidential information discover from a third party that I was not a student. The importance of making known one's identity in this kind of research is illustrated by the following incident, in which, after introducing myself and asking permission to observe, I sat in on the first student government meeting. The field notes describe what happened after that:

> After several motions are unanimously passed four students walk in late. Sue suggests they elect a chairperson.... One of the students who came late nominates me: "I'd like to nominate this gentleman on my left. He looks like he knows what to do." There is a roar of laughter after which the other students explain to him who I am. I thank him for the nomination anyhow and this gets more laughter. If I hadn't explained myself beforehand this would have been a very embarrassing situation for me.

It would, of course, have been more than embarrassing, for had I been forced to unmask myself as an outsider I might well have diminished my chances of becoming trusted.[2]

Participant as Observer

On several occasions I was invited to school-sponsored as well as to private social events. For example, several fire science students asked me to meet them at Sully's (a local bar) on the last day of classes before Christmas vacation, and in this situation the observer role was subordinate to that of participant. My researcher's eyes and ears never were completely closed, for I found myself becoming quite conscious of the way in which I was sociable. Although I wanted to be "natural" I found it impossible, and that the best I could do was devise a performance that hopefully appeared natural. I was not one of them and did not want to attempt to become one of them temporarily, yet not wanting to appear too academic I found myself using profanity for effect but being careful not to overuse it.

I would often play ping-pong, scrabble, and other games with students as well as have lengthy conversations that had little or nothing to do with the investigation. I would almost always be alive to the possibility of important data coming up in these conversations, yet sometimes would purposely not use them to my advantage. Rather than constantly asking questions, I wanted students to feel comfortable with me and so speak spontaneously; when I did ask questions I wanted them to feel free to answer me as they would a friend. In many cases my relationships with students did become quite friendly, and consequently I could never escape the guilt I felt because of these manipulations.

During the many conversations in which some aspect of school was discussed, my usual strategy was not to say anything unless I became confused or thought of some question particularly important to ask. Sometimes these conversations became informal interviews as I asked a student or a group of students a number of questions. Students would also ask my opinion of some teacher or some problem and in this way I was drawn into the discussion as a participant. (The dilemmas of answering these questions are discussed under the role of informant.)

One of the advantages of not wholly concealing my role as observer was that people often sought me out to offer various kinds of information. Many times students would hail me in the hallway or cafeteria to describe an event that happened in class or to urge me to go to a class with them in anticipation of some event. Another advantage of participation was that students who trusted me frequently offered unsolicited and intimate data about themselves and others, commenting that they would not tell these things to others. Thus although a friend and coparticipant, I was also an outside observer and, like Georg Simmel's stranger, often received "the most surprising openness—confidences which sometimes have the character of a confessional and which would be carefully withheld from a more closely related person."[3]

Observer as Participant

In classes and various student meetings I acted primarily as an observer and in some cases had to rebuff attempts by others to draw me into participation. In three classes teachers asked if I knew something about the academic matter being discussed and although I did, I claimed I did not. To answer the question would have meant participating as a colleague of the teacher, which, of course, is not how I wanted to be seen in front of students. For the same reason I had to refuse an invitation to lecture a class on student culture. Perhaps more problematic were the teachers who in the face of students' resistance or apathy attempted to make eye contact with me in search of sympathy. It is not that I did not empathize with them, but, again, I did not want students to see me participating in this fashion. The following describes one such incident:

> A moment later she asked another question about the main idea of the article they had read. Again there was no response. As she had done several times before when there was no response she made eye contact with me. . . . If I read her gestures and mannerisms correctly, she had become progressively flustered. Furthermore, with each successive "failure" her eye contact with me came sooner after the question and stayed slightly longer. This was remedial interaction of the first order; it was as if she was saying, "Look I don't think this passivity is my fault and I do not condone it. I am embarrassed that you have witnessed it and I hope you do not attribute it to a weakness on my part." Finally, I had to purposefully avoid eye contact. I remember thinking that the minute class was over and I began to move from my chair she would interrupt whatever she was doing and ask to see me. . . . Before I was half out of my chair she stopped talking with a student and said to me, "Can I see you for a minute?"

In situations such as these I waited until all students had left the room before reassuring teachers that I was not assessing their ability to draw students into discussions, that I was as concerned as they about the apathy, and that I had witnessed it in other classes as well. During the second semester the frequency of such incidents dropped off sharply as the teachers became accustomed to my presence and as the knowledge spread that student apathy and incivility were indeed problems confronting most teachers.

Another kind of situation in which the observer role was dominant was when having introduced myself as a researcher or having greeted a student I already knew, I was asked something like, "What have you found out?" or "How's the study going?" I found that by answering with a statement such as "OK, I guess, but I'm kind of puzzled about the absenteeism [or some other problem]" that students would then offer their own analyses and thereby set the stage for further questions.

The observer role was also most salient when on occasion students introduced me to their friends as a researcher and would ask them a question for me; like Doc in *Street Corner Society* or Tally in *Tally's Corner*, these students were most helpful as entrees into various cliques and activities.[4]

Complete Observer

The role of complete observer was played on those occasions when I stayed long enough for overhearing to become eavesdropping. For example, sometimes finding myself seated close to students in the lounge but not as part of their group, I would make myself busy by spreading a school catalogue before me and appear to be copying information from it, when in fact I would be taking brief notes on their conversation. I also made it a practice to listen for students' whispered remarks in class and their comments on the way in and out of class. The complete observer role was also used by walking behind or slightly ahead of a group of talking students or sitting behind one of the several walls in the school, which because they did not extend to the ceiling, made it possible to eavesdrop; in this situation I spread papers before me or held a newspaper in my hands should I be seen.

The ethical dilemma here is obvious. Although I was obtaining valuable data, I was doing so without the knowledge or consent of students and teachers. My rationale, that I was harming no one, never expiated all my guilt, for people have a right to be protected from even the benign intentions of others. A related ethical problem was that students and teachers probably did not know I would later write up the conversations they had with me or the behavior they exhibited before me. Although when I described the study I always made it a point to say that the school and the people in it would remain anonymous, I never revealed that conversations and behavior were being recorded as best I could remember them. In short, subjects were not fully informed of the extent to which I was an observer. This duplicity was unquestionably the most distasteful part of the fieldwork.

Informant

Students, teachers, and administrators would occasionally ask me to analyze various school problems, such as absenteeism, apathy, or the "down" feeling they thought pervaded the school. During the first semester and for the first half of the second semester I avoided answering these questions by saying, usually honestly, that I too was puzzled. During the last month I offered tentative explanations to a few of my best student informants (not to teachers because I had not yet taped interviews with them), carefully explaining the relationship between social class and the student culture.

There were two reasons for doing this. First, to deny that I had even tentative conclusions would probably be disbelieved and might be seen as a violation of the trust some students had placed in me. Second, it was thought at the time to be a good method of confirming or disconfirming my analyses. In every case except one students agreed with my analyses, sometimes enthusiastically offering examples to support a point. In retrospect, I may have too heavily influenced their responses to rely on them as checks of validity, hence only the more spontaneous data were used in this report.

Several times during the year I was asked for my opinion of a teacher by another teacher or by a student. When asked by a teacher I would explain that it would set a bad precedent to discuss such things, and that I would prefer not to comment. When asked by students I gave a favorable response if I sensed they liked the teacher in question, and simply made a face indicating displeasure if they disliked the teacher. Not wanting others to repeat anything negative I might have to say about a teacher or student, I gave them nothing to quote.

Adviser

Several students asked me for advice on such matters as course selections, course loads, transferring to senior colleges, making the student government more effective, career choices, and a host of personal, nonacademic problems. Academic advice was usually based on the answers to questions I would put to students, trying to uncover their own desires. The suggestion that they talk with one of the student counselors was usually dismissed. Personal advice was more difficult and required lengthy and often emotional conversations with students. It was a role I would rather not have played, but could not in good conscience refuse. I felt that I owed something to these students for letting me into their world, and if I had a chance to repay them I should do so.

SAMPLING

At the beginning of the year the courses I attended were randomly selected. Since each course met at a designated time (for example, 11:00 A.M. on Tuesday), each was given a number that in turn was picked from a box, the selections being made one day in advance. I tried to attend a minimum of three courses per day. Sometimes my schedule was upset by a student or teacher inviting me to his class or by involvement in a conversation too interesting to leave. After about eight weeks, as I gradually became conscious of the different perspectives of different groups of students, I began spending several hours and sometimes one to three days with one group of students (for example, younger male liberal arts students) before moving on to another group (for example, older students).[5]

A minor difficulty of this method was the awkwardness of being seen in the company of one group by students with whom I had spent the previous day(s); moving from clique to clique, I feared being seen as having switched allegiances, although I never heard any such accusations. There were occasions, for example, when a student would see me with a student or group of students he had vilified earlier, or with a teacher for whom he had expressed a particular distaste. As a general rule I avoided as much as possible being seen with teachers (usually meeting with them in the faculty lounge), and on several occasions found it necessary to hide from administrators for fear they would say hello, or worst of all, ask embarrassing questions in front of students.

In addition to classes and groups, I also sampled various settings by placing myself in several locations where students congregated, such as the game room, the lounges, and the hallways. I usually did this on one of three occasions: when after jotting down field notes (see below) the next class had not yet begun; when students with whom I had been talking decided to go home; or when students would go to a class I did not want to attend. I also spent several hours each week informally talking with teachers in the faculty lounge; it was necessary to visit their lounge at different times of the day to ensure contact with different teachers. Appendix A depicts the design of City Community College and the location of these settings.

FIELD NOTES

Throughout the year I carried a small easily concealed notebook in which, using my own idiosyncratic shorthand, I jotted down my observations and reconstructed conversations. Note taking was usually done in a place where I would not be detected or in a manner in which I would not be suspected. The men's room was one spot to record brief notes, although I always felt a bit ridiculous sitting on the toilet writing up my observations. The most frequent location was a wing of the school not yet opened to students, where, having made an arrangement with workmen, I recorded my notes in a secluded classroom.

To remember important points from students' classes I would often take very brief notes while doodling. For example, to record the seating arrangement I would make a series of "Xs" and "Os" to designate males and females; to help reconstruct a dialog I would write key words or letters on a slip of paper or a book jacket while appearing to be nonchalantly perusing the room. Similarly, during conversations with students I would sometimes doodle and let them have a view of the doodle, yet hidden in it were symbols to help me recall as faithfully as possible what was said. Despite these occasional aids, I relied primarily on concentration and memory. Indeed, at the end of most days I was exhausted from these efforts and it was all I could do that evening to round out the notes. Although the reconstructions of students' comments in this report are not always verbatim, every effort has been made to convey the original meaning of what was said. In the last two months of field work I occasionally took brief notes in class in a City Community College notebook. I finally accumulated over 1,000 pages of field notes (excluding interviews with teachers).

The first days in the field were especially exhausting and confusing because, seeing no patterns and not knowing what later might be significant, I tried to absorb as much as possible. In most cases my insights came from rereading the field notes in the quiet of my home. For example, the relationship between social class and the fear of success did not dawn on me until I reviewed the following account:

> As I have repeatedly recorded, most students wear blue jeans, faded blue jeans. To paraphrase Janis Joplin, I cannot help but feel that many of the students are as faded as their jeans. Many of the students work until the late hours, many have dismal academic records, many are here because the school represents a second, third, or last chance to change their lot; much of their laughter is hollow.... So many students here seem so deadly serious—not about their schoolwork because they tell me they study very little—but about their lives. This in itself is paradoxical. They are concerned but they see little need for study. There are some exceptions; I have met a few students (especially the firemen) who laugh easily, who enjoy school, who just seem to be more alive to their surroundings and have a greater sense of confidence and personal efficacy. But most students are more fatalistic or else seem to be wandering. It is probably a good thing to wander at some point in one's life, but they wander without wonder; there is no joy in their eyes. I do sometimes feel depressed in the school; I think I feel that way because it saddens me that so many students seem to be already worn out—even though most of them are only in their late teens or early twenties. They appear to have already had their moments of glory.

It had bothered me for some time that the "faded hypothesis" (as I came to call it) seemed so nebulous and impressionistic. As I read further that evening I came across some accounts of students upsetting their teachers; at first I had thought these incivilities to be little more than rude and aggressive humor, but suddenly I saw the possibility that these encounters expressed an anxiety related to the paradox and the mood I had described earlier. Looking through my notes for more incidents of hostility I came across the phrase "middle-class teachers" and it struck me that if students were in fact apprehensive and limiting their effort in a seemingly irrational manner, then perhaps this was related to their socioeconomic status. I had assumed all along that the desire for upward mobility was relatively uncomplicated; but now I wondered if I indeed was guilty of a serious oversight. I scribbled a one-line note to myself, "SES anxiety in humor?" still not certain that I was on a correct course, but at least now with something for which to look.

As I was to discover from this beginning, social class was a central component of students' perspectives. In the methodological appendix to *Street Corner Society*, William Foote Whyte eloquently summarizes this process of discovery and, implicitly, the importance of good field notes:

> The ideas that we have in research are only in part a logical product growing out of a careful weighing of evidence. . . . We study the data carefully, bringing all our powers of logical analysis to bear upon them. We come up with an idea or two. But still the data do not fall into any coherent pattern. Then we go on living with the data—and with the people—until perhaps some chance occurrence casts a totally different light upon the data, and we begin to see a pattern we did not see before. This pattern is not purely an artistic creation. Once we think we see it, we must re-examine our notes and perhaps set out to gather new data in order to determine whether the pattern adequately represents the life we are observing or is simply a product of our imagination. Logic, then, plays an important part. But I am convinced that the actual evaluation of research ideas does not take place in accord with the formal statements we read on research methods. The ideas grow up in part out of our immersion in the data and out of the whole process of living.[6]

Approximately six weeks before the conclusion of the fieldwork, I content-analyzed my notes and cataloged on index cards 51 sometimes overlapping categories of phenomena.[7] Ideally, I should have done this sooner, but in weighing my desire to obtain as many data as possible against the time it would take to analyze the notes, I postponed the content analysis until I felt I no longer was picking up anything new in the field. In the following weeks I set aside time to concentrate on those few categories with insufficient data. For example, I discovered that I had talked with relatively few older liberal arts students and that to confirm the observation that they were more willing to intellectualize I needed to spend more time with them.

TAPE-RECORDED INTERVIEWS

Tape-recorded interviews of teachers were begun four weeks before the end of the second semester and continued until the last day of fieldwork. A representative group of 25 teachers was selected on the basis of age and sex, as well as what I already knew of their educational and occupational histories. Twelve more teachers were also interviewd, but, no longer learning anything new, it hardly seemed worthwhile to continue after these 37. Interviews were requested several days in advance and each teacher was reminded the day before the interview. No teachers refused to be interviewed, although two declined being recorded. In asking for an interview I simply stated that as part of the study I wanted to question them on their educational and occupational backgrounds, as well on their thoughts on community college teaching. Because teachers did not have offices, I also told them that I had arranged to use an empty classroom where we could talk in privacy. While escorting teachers from their desks to the interview, I asked permission to use the tape recorder, explaining that I would be the only one to hear the tape and that after transcription it would be erased.

The interviews consisted of a series of open-ended questions (see Appendix B), some of which were modified slightly to suit the chemistry and idiosyncracies of each interview. The chief problem in the interviews was the sensitive nature of the questions concerning the career transition and how successfully or unsuccessfully it had been made. Because I had previously suspected that some teachers' careers had taken an unanticipated and unwelcomed turn, I wanted to allow for the development of that line of thought without being bound to it. My strategy, then, was to begin with a few simple background questions on age and social class (questions 1-4), followed by questions concerning the chronologies and contingencies of their aspirations and careers (5-13). The next set of questions (14-24) concerned the problematic features of the work role and their assessments of students, and, finally, the last question explored how teachers viewed their present work and themselves in light of their experiences.

As I began asking about the discrepancy between expectations and reality, I often sensed that teachers knew what I was getting at—that we were discussing or about to discuss the extent to which their careers had soured. Having seen me in their classes and having talked with me during the year, they knew I was familiar with their work problems, and many of them did reveal intimate thoughts. In three interviews I had the unverifiable feeling that teachers were not being honest and that there was nothing I could do to uncover the truth. In six interviews, however, I was told after the tape recorder had been switched off that thoughts and feelings were expressed they would not have shared even with colleagues. Indeed, some interviews did seem cathartic for teachers, as if they now had an opportunity to discuss something previously kept secret; these observations were also unverifiable, as they were based on those signs of emotion (eye contact, voice, mannerisms) that in the interest of ethics and good taste I dared not question.

NOTES

1. Raymond L. Gold, "Roles in Sociological Field Observations," *Social Forces* 36 (February 1958): 217-23.

2. Examples of studies in which sociologists used false identities are Laud Humphreys, *Tearoom Trade* (Chicago: Aldine, 1970); and Leon Festinger et al., *When Prophecy Fails* (New York: Harper & Row, 1956).

3. Georg Simmel, "The Stranger," in *The Sociology of Georg Simmel,* ed. Kurt Wolff (New York: Free Press, 1950), p. 404.

4. William Foote Whyte, *Street Corner Society,* 2d ed. (Chicago: University of Chicago Press, 1955), pp. 298-302; Elliot Liebow, *Tally's Corner* (Boston: Little, Brown, 1967), p. 240.

5. For a discussion of sampling techniques in qualitative research, see Barney G. Glaser and Anselm L. Strauss, *The Discovery of Grounded Theory* (Chicago: Aldine, 1970), Ch. 3, pp. 45-78.

6. Whyte, *Street Corner Society,* pp. 279-80.

7. See Ole R. Holsti, *Content Analysis for the Social Sciences and the Humanities* (Reading, Mass.: Addison-Wesley, 1969), Ch. 5, pp. 94-126.

APPENDIX B
FLOOR PLAN OF
CITY COMMUNITY COLLEGE,
FIRST AND SECOND FLOORS

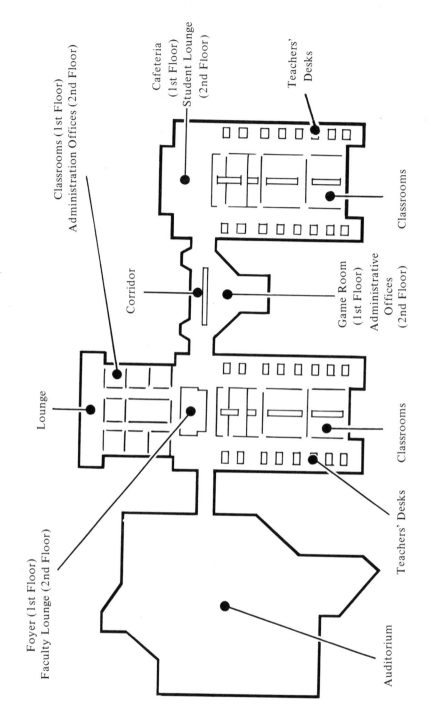

Classrooms (1st Floor)
Administration Offices (2nd Floor)

Cafeteria
(1st Floor)
Student Lounge
(2nd Floor)

Teachers'
Desks

Corridor

Classrooms

Game Room
(1st Floor)
Administrative
Offices
(2nd Floor)

Lounge

Classrooms

Foyer (1st Floor)
Faculty Lounge (2nd Floor)

Teachers' Desks

Auditorium

APPENDIX C
THE QUESTIONNAIRE SCHEDULE

THE QUESTIONNAIRE SCHEDULE

Note: This schedule was used as an informal quide. Most teachers were asked additional exploratory questions depending on the content of their answers.

1. Sex
2. Age
3. Parents' Education
4. Parents' Occupations (specifically)
5. Interested in your education and occupational history—List all schools attended and job experiences in chronological order beginning with high school graduation. (How long at each, degrees earned, field of study.)
6. Eliminating the quixotic did you ever have any concrete career plans that due to one circumstance or another were changed? (Probes: In your earlier days—say after you graduated from college—what did you see as your ideal future—if everything went your way?)
7. Interested in circumstances and events which brought you to your first community college teaching job. When did you first begin to think of teaching in a community college? (Age, personal family situation?)
8. Were there any crucial points of decision where you could have chosen another path?
9. Were there people who you consulted or advised you or acted as sponsors concerning your first job in a community college? (Who? Nature of their advice? Reactions of friends, family, past colleagues?)
10. How did you actually get first job? Succeeding jobs? This job?
11. What were your immediate plans just before becoming aware you might teach in a community college? What would you have done if there was no prospect of teaching in a community college, if no jobs were available?
12. Would you like to move on to another position at some time in future? To what? Why? What inhibits your moving on?
13. Would you someday like to teach in a four-year college (If not already answered, did they ever?)

14. FOR FACULTY WHO HAVE TAUGHT AT OTHER COMMU-
NITY COLLEGES: Interested in comparing your expectations before your first experience in a community college and what you
actually found. Did you have any difficulties orienting yourself to
the community college? If not already answered: Change number
of readings? Difficulty of readings and other course work? Social
class of other schools' students?

15. What differences do you see between your vocational students and
your nonvocational students? (Not applicable to all teachers.) Probes: Do you find yourself approaching them differently in any way?
In ways you teach them? In ways they respond to you? What
problems do you have in teaching either of these groups? How do
you resolve them? Differences in academic ability? Willingness?

16. Differences between older and younger students?

17. Differences between male and female students?

18. Do you have any problems in grading students? How resolved? Do
these problems vary by whether students vocational or nonvocational?

19. Do you derive more intrinsic satisfaction teaching either vocational
or nonvocational students? Explain. Why do you think this is?

20. How do you define success in teaching at a community college such
as this one?

21. What prevents you from being as successful as you would like to
be in this position? (Probes: Do students make it very difficult and
frustrating for you to do what you would like to do or do they make
it relatively easy and comfortable? In what ways?)

22. What is there that you especially like about teaching in a community college?

23. Do not like? How do you handle it?

24. What do you see as the essential differences (if any) between the
community college and four-year colleges? Explain.

25. This last question is perhaps a bit sensitive and I'd like you to
respond to it as openly as possible. Do you ever have to rationalize
to yourself why you are here? (If asked to explain: Do you have to
give yourself reasons for teaching here, but you can't really believe
in those reasons?) Explore.

BIBLIOGRAPHY

Aronowitz, Stanley. *False Promises: The Shaping of Working Class Consciousness.* New York: McGraw-Hill, 1973.

Becker, Howard S. "Problems of Inference and Proof in Participant Observation." *American Sociological Review* 23 (1958): 652–60.

———. "Notes on the Concept of Commitment." *American Journal of Sociology* 66, no. 1 (July 1960): 32–48.

———. *Sociological Work: Method and Substance.* Chicago: Aldine, 1970.

Becker, Howard S., and Carper, James. "The Elements of Identification with an Occupation." *American Sociological Review* 21 (June 1956): 341–48.

———, and ———. "The Development of Identification with an Occupation." *American Journal of Sociology* 61 (January 1956): 289–98.

Becker, Howard S.; Geer, Blanche; Hughes, Everett; and Strauss, Anselm. *Boys in White: Student Culture in Medical School.* Chicago: University of Chicago Press, 1961.

Becker, Howard S.; Geer, Blanche; and Hughes, Everett. *Making the Grade.* New York: Wiley, 1968.

Becker, Howard S., and Strauss, Anselm. "Careers, Personality and Adult Socialization." *American Journal of Sociology* 62 (November 1965): 253–63.

Berger, Peter L., and Luckmann, Thomas. *The Social Construction of Reality: A Treatise in the Sociology of Knowledge.* Garden City, N.Y.: Doubleday, 1969.

Binstock, Jeanne. "Design from Disunity: The Tasks and Methods of American Colleges." Ph.D. dissertation, Brandeis University, 1970.

Binzen, Peter. *Whitetown, U.S.A.* New York: Random House, 1970.

Blocker, Clyde E.; Plummer, Robert H.; and Richardson, Richard C. *The Two-Year College: A Social Synthesis.* Englewood Cliffs, N.J.: Prentice-Hall, 1965.

Blum, Fred H. "Getting Individuals to Give Information to the Outsider." *Journal of Social Issues* 8, no. 3 (1952): 35–42.

Blumer, Herbert. "Sociological Implications of the Thought of George Herbert Mead." *American Journal of Sociology* 61 (March 1966): 535–44.

_____. *Symbolic Interactionism: Perspective and Method.* Englewood Cliffs, N.J.: Prentice-Hall, 1969.

Brick, Michael. *Forum and Focus for the Junior College Movement.* New York: Bureau of Publications, Teachers College, Columbia University, 1964.

Bruyn, Severyn T. *The Human Perspective in Sociology: The Methodology of Participant Observation.* Englewood Cliffs, N.J.: Prentice-Hall, 1966.

Bucher, Rue, and Strauss, Anselm. "Professions in Process." *American Journal of Sociology* 66 (January 1961): 325–34.

Carnegie Commission on Higher Education. *The Open Door Colleges. A Special Report and Recommendation by the Carnegie Commission on Higher Education.* New York: McGraw-Hill, 1970.

Chenowith, Lawrence. *The American Dream of Success: The Search for Self in the Twentieth Century.* Belmont, Calif.: Wadsworth, 1974.

Clark, Burton. *The Open Door College.* New York: McGraw-Hill, 1960.

_____. "The 'Cooling-Out' Function in Higher Education." *American Journal of Sociology* 65 (May 1960): 269–76.

Cohen, Arthur M., et al. *A Constant Variable: New Perspectives on the Community College.* San Francisco: Jossey-Bass, 1971.

Cohen, Arthur M., and Brawer, Florence B. *Confronting Identity: The Community College Instructor.* Englewood Cliffs, N.J.: Prentice-Hall, 1972.

Cross, K. Patricia. *The Junior College Students: A Research Description.* Princeton, N.J.: Educational Testing Service, 1968.

_____. *Beyond the Open Door.* San Francisco: Jossey-Bass, 1972.

Dean, John, and Whyte, William F. "How Do You Know if the Informant Is Telling the Truth?" *Human Organization* 17, no. 2 (1958): 34–38.

Dean, John, et al. "Establishing Field Relations." In *Issues in Participant Observations.* Edited by George McCall and J. L. Simmons. Reading, Mass.: Addison-Wesley, 1969.

Deutsch, Morton; Krauss, R. M.; and Rosenau, Norah. "Dissonance or Defensiveness." *Journal of Personality* 60 (1962): 16–28.

Dexter, Lewis Anthony. *The Tyranny of Schooling*. New York: Basic Books, 1964.

Dibble, Vernon K. "Occupations and Ideologies." *American Journal of Sociology* 68 (September 1962): 229–41.

Diekhoff, John S. *Democracy's College*. New York: Harper & Row, 1950.

Emerson, Joan. "Behavior in Private Places: Sustaining Definitions of Reality in Gynecological Examinations." In *Recent Sociology*, no. 2. Edited by Hans Peter Dreitzel. New York: Macmillan, 1970.

Faulkner, Robert R. *Hollywood Studio Musicians: Their Work and Careers in the Recording Industry*. Chicago: Aldine/Atherton, 1971.

Glaser, Barney. *Organizational Careers: A Sourcebook for Theory*. Chicago: Aldine, 1968.

——, and Strauss, Anselm L. *The Discovery of Grounded Theory: Strategies for Qualitative Research*. Chicago: Aldine, 1967.

Gleazer, Edmund J., Jr. *American Junior Colleges*. 8th ed. Washington, D.C.: American Council on Education, 1971.

Goffman, Erving. *Asylums*. Garden City, N.Y.: Doubleday, 1961.

Gold, Raymond L. "Roles in Sociological Field Observations." *Social Forces* 36 (February 1958): 217–23.

Goldner, Fred. "Professionalization as Career Immobility." *American Journal of Sociology* 72 (March 1967): 489–502.

Gornick, Vivian. "Why Women Fear Success." In *Current Perspectives on Social Problems*. Edited by Judson R. Landis. Belmont, Calif.: Wadsworth, 1973.

Haslocker, Ervin L. *The Community Dimension of the Community College*. Englewood Cliffs, N.J.: Prentice-Hall, 1969.

Havighurst, Robert J., and Neugarten, Bernice L. *Society and Education*. 3d ed. Boston: Allyn & Bacon, 1967.

Holsti, Ole R. *Content Analysis for the Social Sciences and Humanities*. Reading, Mass.: Addison-Wesley, 1969.

Horner, Matina. "Femininity and Successful Achievement: A Basic Inconsistency." In *Feminine Personality and Conflict*. Edited by Judith M. Burdwick et al. Belmont, Calif.: Wadsworth, 1970.

Hughes, Everett C. "Institutional Office and the Person." *American Journal of Sociology* 43 (November 1937): 404–13.

_____. "The Sociological Study of Work: An Editorial Forward." *American Journal of Sociology* 57 (March 1952): 423–26.

_____. *Men and Their Work.* Glencoe, Ill.: Free Press, 1958.

_____. "Non-Economic Aspects of Academic Morale." In *Higher Education in the United States.* Edited by Seymore E. Harris. Cambridge, Mass.: Harvard University Press, 1960.

_____. *Students—Culture and Perspectives: Lectures on Medical and General Education.* Lawrence, Kans.: University of Kansas Press, 1961.

_____. "The Study of Occupations." In *The Sociological Eye: Selected Papers.* Chicago: Aldine/Atherton, 1971.

_____. "Work and Self." In *The Sociological Eye: Selected Papers.* Chicago: Aldine/Atherton, 1971.

_____. "Careers." Unpublished paper. No date.

Hyman, Hubert H. "The Value Systems of Different Classes: A Social Psychological Contribution to the Analysis of Stratification." In *Class, Status and Power.* 2d ed. Edited by Reinhard Bendix and Seymour Lipset. Glencoe, Ill.: Free Press, 1966.

Ichheiser, Gustav. "Toward a Psychology of Success." In *Appearances and Realities: Misunderstandings in Human Relations.* San Francisco: Jossey-Bass, 1970.

Jencks, Christopher, and Riesman, David. *The Academic Revolution.* Garden City, N.Y.: Doubleday, 1968.

Kahl, Joseph. *The American Class Structure.* New York: Holt, Rinehart and Winston, 1965.

Karabel, Jerome. "Protecting the Portals: Class and the Community College." *Social Policy* (May/June 1974): 12–18.

Katz, Joseph. "Personality and Interpersonal Relations in the College Classroom." In *The American College: A Psychological and Social Interpretation of the Higher Learning.* Edited by Nevitt Sanford. New York: Wiley, 1962.

Katz, Michael B. *Class, Bureaucracy and Schools.* New York: Praeger, 1971.

Kempton, Murray, "Blue Collar Blues." *New York Review of Books* (February 8, 1973), pp. 11–15.

Klotsche, J. Martin. *The Urban University.* New York: Harper & Row, 1966.

Komarovsky, Mirra. "Functional Analysis of Sex Roles." *American Sociological Review* 15 (August 1950): 508–16.

Koos, Leonard V. *The Community College Student.* Gainesville, Fla.: University of Florida Press, 1970.

Lasch, Christopher. "Inequality and Education." *New York Review of Books* (May 17, 1973), pp. 19–25.

Lazarsfeld, Paul. *Qualitative Analysis: Historical and Critical Essays.* Boston: Allyn & Bacon, 1972.

Liebow, Elliot. *Tally's Corner: A Study of Negro Streetcorner Men.* Boston: Little, Brown, 1967.

Lofland, John. *Analyzing Social Settings.* Belmont, Calif.: Wadsworth, 1971.

McDermott, John. "The Laying-On of Culture." *Nation,* March 10, 1969, pp. 296–301.

Mannheim, Karl. *Ideology and Utopia.* New York: Harcourt, Brace, 1936.

Martorana, S. V.; Toombs, William; and Breveman, David W., eds. *Graduate Education and Community Colleges.* A Technical Report Presented to the National Board on Graduate Education. Washington, D.C.: National Board on Graduate Education, 1975.

Mead, Margaret. *The School in American Culture.* Cambridge: Harvard University Press, 1964.

Medsker, Leland L. *The Junior College: Progress and Prospect.* New York: McGraw-Hill, 1960.

———. "Changes in Junior Colleges and Technical Institutes." In *Emerging Patterns in Higher Education.* Edited by Logan Wilson. Washington, D.C.: American Council on Education, 1965.

———, and Tillery, Dale. *Breaking the Access Barriers: A Profile of the American Junior College.* New York: McGraw-Hill, 1971.

Mills, C. Wright. *White Collar: The American Middle Class.* New York: Oxford University Press, 1956.

_____. *The Sociological Imagination.* New York: Oxford University Press, 1959.

Monroe, Charles R. *Profile of the Community College.* San Francisco: Jossey-Bass, 1972.

Moore, William, Jr. *Against the Odds: The High Risk Student in the Community College.* San Francisco: Jossey-Bass, 1970.

Newcomb, Theodore M., and Wilson, Everett K., eds. *College Peer Groups.* Chicago: Aldine, 1966.

O'Connell, Thomas E. *Community Colleges: A President's View.* Urbana: University of Illinois Press, 1968.

Reiss, Albert J. *Occupations and Social Status.* New York: Free Press, 1961.

Reynolds, James W. *The Junior College.* New York: Center for Applied Research in Education, 1965.

Riesman, David. *Constraint and Variety in American Education.* Garden City, N.Y.: Doubleday, 1956.

_____; Gusfield, Joseph; and Gamson, Zelda. *Academic Values and Mass Education.* Garden City, N.Y.: Doubleday, 1970.

Robinson, W. S. "Ecological Correlations and the Behavior of Individuals." *American Sociological Review* 15 (June 1950): 351–57.

Roth, Julius. "Comments on Secret Observation." *Social Problems* 9, no. 3 (1962): 283–84.

Roueche, John E., and Boggs, John R. *Junior College Institutional Research: The State of the Art.* Washington, D.C.: American Association of Junior Colleges, 1968.

Ryan, William. *Blaming the Victim.* New York: Random House, 1971.

Sennett, Richard, and Cobb, Jonathan. *The Hidden Injuries of Class.* New York: Random House, 1972.

Shibutani, Tamotsu. "Reference Groups as Perspectives." *American Journal of Sociology* 60 (May 1955): 562–69.

Shinn, Ronald. *Culture and School.* Scranton, Pa.: Intext Educational Publishers, 1972.

Simmel, Georg. "The Web of Group Affiliations." In *Conflict and the Web of Group Affiliations*. Translated by Kurt Wolff. New York: Free Press, 1955.

Strauss, Anselm, ed. *George Herbert Mead on Social Psychology*. Chicago: University of Chicago Press, 1964.

Sudnow, David. *Passing On: The Social Organization of Dying*. Englewood Cliffs, N.J.: Prentice-Hall, 1967.

Sumner, William Graham. *Folkways*. Boston: Ginn, 1906.

Sutherland, Edwin. *Principles of Criminology*. Revised by D. R. Cressey. Chicago: Lippincott, 1955.

Thornton, James W. *The Community Junior College*. Wiley, 1960.

Trow, Martin. "The Transition from Mass to Universal Higher Education." *Daedalus* (Winter 1970): 1–42.

Turner, Ralph. "Role-Taking: Process Versus Conformity." In *Human Behavior and Social Process*. Edited by Arnold M. Rose. Boston: Houghton Mifflin, 1962.

Vidich, Arthur J. "Participant Observation and the Collection and Interpretation of Data." *American Journal of Sociology* 60 (January 1965): 354–60.

Waller, Willard. *The Sociology of Teaching*. New York: Wiley, 1932.

Wax, Rosalie. *Doing Fieldwork: Warnings and Advice*. Chicago: University of Chicago Press, 1971.

Weber, Max. *Economy and Society*. Edited by Guenther Ross and Claus Wittich. New York: Bedminster Press, 1968.

Whyte, William Foote. *Street Corner Society*. Chicago: University of Chicago Press, 1943.

_____. "Interviewing in Field Research." In *Human Organization Research*. Edited by Richard N. Adams and Jack J. Preiss. Homewood, Ill.: Dorsey Press, 1960.

Zelditch, Morris. "Some Methodological Problems of Field Studies." *American Journal of Sociology* 67 (1962): 566–76.

ABOUT THE AUTHOR

HOWARD B. LONDON received his undergraduate degree from Bowdoin College and his M.A. and Ph.D. in sociology from Boston College. He teaches in the Department of Sociology, Tulane University, New Orleans, Louisiana.

RELATED TITLES
Published by
Praeger Special Studies